# *The* BIBLE TIMELINE
## *guided* JOURNAL

### THE GREAT ADVENTURE

*Sarah Christmyer*

This guided journal follows
*The Great Adventure Bible Timeline*
90-day Bible reading plan

## ASCENSION
West Chester, Pennsylvania

*The Bible Timeline Guided Journal* is a resource of *The Great Adventure* Bible Study Program.

Ascension
Post Office Box 1990
West Chester, PA 19380
1-800-376-0520
ascensionpress.com

Cover design by Devin Schadt

Printed in the United States of America

ISBN 978-1-934217-16-0

*This* JOURNAL *Belongs to*:

_____

_____

DATE *Begun*:

_____

# *90-Day* READING PLAN *at a Glance*

# CONTENTS

# The PURPOSE *of this* JOURNAL

This journal, which is based on *The Bible Timeline* learning system from *The Great Adventure*, is designed to help people read through the story of salvation history as it is found in the Bible. It follows *The Bible Timeline*'s ninety-day reading plan: covering four chapters a day, it guides readers through 14 books of the Bible that, when read consecutively, tell that story from start to finish. By reading these together, you can get the "big picture," a narrative context in which to read the rest of the Bible.

Many thousands of people have read through the biblical story with the help of this reading plan since Jeff Cavins first developed it in 1984. The purpose of this guided journal is to help and encourage those who would otherwise have trouble sticking to a reading plan or who find themselves getting stuck when they don't understand something or lose track of the story.

Here's how it works:

- The "narrative books" of *The Bible Timeline* are divided into ninety daily readings of about four chapters each.[1]

- These readings are then grouped into twelve historic time periods. Each period is introduced by a synopsis and a list of key people and events.

- There are two pages for each day's reading assignment, with room to write down things to remember, questions to come back to, and a prayerful response to God. Brief questions and comments on each page help you focus on the people and events that move the story forward and sometimes clarify concepts or highlight links between a passage and its fulfillment in Christ.

I hope this journal will help you get that "big picture" of God's plan and launch you into a lifetime of reading from His Word!

—Sarah Christmyer

---

[1] The fourteen narrative books are: Genesis, Exodus, Numbers, Joshua, Judges, I and II Samuel, I and II Kings, Ezra, Nehemiah, I Maccabees, Luke, and Acts.

# *How to* USE *this* JOURNAL

1.  Decide how quickly you want to read through the story. Most of the days in this journal assign four chapters of reading, but you can read less or more according to your schedule.

2.  Set aside a regular time and place to read. It takes on average twenty minutes to read four chapters. Allow yourself a good half-hour or more so you can pray and write in your journal as well.

3.  The reading assignments are divided into sections according to the period of Bible history they belong to. Each new section begins with an introduction to the period and highlights the name of the narrative book that tells its story (and that you are about to read), a key verse from that book, and information like the color and dates and key people and events. When appropriate, this introduction will also give you hints on what to watch for or will explain concepts or customs that will help make sense of the reading.

4.  Beginning with Day 1 in the journal, fill in the date and check off the chapters listed at the top of the page as you read them. You can also check off the periods as you complete them on the "Reading Plan at a Glance" that precedes this introduction.

5.  Pray before you read that the Holy Spirit will open your heart and mind to His Word.

6.  Each day's journal entry provides space for you to write in. There are also several questions or comments on each page. Use them to guide your reading as they are helpful, but do not feel bound by them.

7.  Three icons divide each journal entry into sections:

**Remember this**: This area is for notes on what the reading was about. If you do this consistently, you will have at the end a summary of the story in your own words. Keep it simple: not every detail, but the main people and events. Ask yourself the old series of questions, Who? What? When? Where? How? Why? Your goal is simply to note how the story has been advanced in the reading.

**Questions I have**: This is a kind of "holding tank" for things you wonder about or that trouble you so you can go back to them later. Write them here or use the space to reflect on the questions at the top of the page.

**My prayer response**: In the Bible, God speaks to us. In prayer, we reply. Pick one thing you understand from the reading. It might be an attribute of God you want to honor, a lesson to apply in your own life, or something else that spoke to you. It might be a hard question or even something that disturbs you. Whatever it is, prayerfully consider it and offer a prayer back to the Author.

8.  Before you start, read through the "Overview of Bible Periods" on page x. It will take you quickly through the story, describing each period and telling you how to remember it using *The Bible Timeline's* color-coded memory system.

You might want to keep a copy of the *Bible Timeline* chart in your journal for easy reference.

Blessings on you as you read!

# Overview *of* BIBLE PERIODS *and* EXPLANATION *of* COLOR MEMORY SYSTEM

1. In the **Early World**, God created the heavens and Earth and tested Adam and Eve in the garden. This period is represented by the color **turquoise**, which is the color of the earth seen from space.

2. In the time of the **Patriarchs**, God called Abraham and promised his children land, a royal kingdom, and worldwide blessing. The color **burgundy** helps us remember the blood covenant God made with him.

3. In **Egypt and Exodus,** God freed His people from slavery so they could worship Him. **Red** reminds us of the crossing of the Red Sea.

4. God taught Israel to trust Him through forty years of **Desert Wanderings**. What better way to remember those miles of sand than by the color **tan**?

5. In **Conquest and Judges**, God led Israel triumphantly in the Promised Land, represented by **green** for the lush hills of Canaan.

6. There He established Israel as a **Royal Kingdom** under David, who was promised an eternal throne. The color **purple** represents royalty.

7. Israel soon split into rival kingdoms and fell into idolatry. **Black** represents the darkness of this **Divided Kingdom**.

8. God punished both kingdoms with **Exile; baby blue** recalls the children of Judah "singing the blues" in "Baby-lon."

9. Brighter days of **Return** are shown by **yellow**: God brought the exiles home to make a fresh start.

10. Years later, the Maccabees stood up against the threats of Hellenization in the **Maccabean Revolt**.  The color **orange** calls to mind the lit oil lamps in the purified Temple.

11. **Gold** represents the first New Testament period, the time of **Messianic Fulfillment**:  when God at last sent His only son, Jesus Christ the Messiah, to fulfill all His promises.  Remember gold by the gifts of the Magi.

12. Finally, **the Church** carries on God's work in the world.  Its color is **white**, for the spotless Bride of Christ.

# *Staying* FOCUSED

One of the hardest things to do when you are reading through the Bible to get an overview of the story is to stay focused. You are bound to run into things you don't understand or things you want to know more about. If you read with the goal of taking it all in at once or of understanding everything, you will be frustrated. It may help to remember two things:

1. *You have the rest of your life to get the details.* This is not just any book, it is the word of God. The Bible has proved to be deep and rich enough to keep some of the world's best minds going for a lifetime.

2. *It's OK to have questions.* Remember that getting the big picture up front will help you make sense of the pieces later on. Having questions will also keep you coming back for more. We've included space on each journal page for you to keep track of them, for just that purpose.

One way to think about what you are doing is to consider the way an artist paints a mural. He or she never starts on one side and paints across to the other. Rather, they first chalk out the main lines of the composition, then paint a very pale "underpainting" of several colors over the whole thing. It doesn't look good, but that doesn't matter: its purpose it to lay a foundation for the rest. Next the mid-tones go on, then the shadows and finally the highlights. To apply this to *The Bible Timeline*, the seminar lecture chalks out the main lines of the composition: the twelve periods, the people and events. Your first read-through provides the underpainting. Mid-tones and shadows and highlights will come as you read more and study. The "painting"—your understanding of Scripture—will get more and more detailed as time goes on.

If you forget this and get frustrated as you read, you are not alone. It's human nature to want to understand. But none of us will ever get to the end of the Bible. That's the beauty of it! So sit back, and try to get that underpainting done. It may not be pretty, but it will help form a good foundation for the reading you do for the rest of your life.

---

"READ DAILY,
and thence gather food for your soul.
—*Spiritus Paracletus*, 43.

---

# EARLY WORLD

*Turquoise*

"In the beginning God created the heavens and the earth" (Gen. 1:1).

"The LORD God said to the serpent, "Because you have done this,
. . . I will put enmity between you and the woman, and between
your seed and her seed; he shall bruise your head, and you shall
bruise his heel" (Gen. 3:14-15).

# INTRODUCTION *to the* EARLY WORLD

◇ ◆ ◆ ◆ ◆ ◆ ◆ ◆ ◆ ◆ ◆ ◆

**Narrative book:** Genesis 1-11

**Color:** Turquoise / the color of the Earth seen from space

**Key people and events:**

- Creation of Earth and Adam and Eve     Gen. 1-2
- Fall     Gen. 3
- Curse and promise (*protoevangelium*)     Gen. 3:8-24
- Noah and the Flood     Gen. 6-9
- People scattered at Babel     Gen. 11:1-9

The first eleven chapters of Genesis, which describe the *Early World* period of Bible history, contain some of the best-known stories in the Bible—Creation, Adam and Eve, Cain and Abel, Noah, the Tower of Babel. It is here that the Story starts and where it finds its roots: "in the beginning," with God creating the heavens and the Earth. These stories set the stage for the rest of the story, and the rest doesn't make sense without them.

A great deal of time and energy has gone into the debate of whether these stories are history or myth. Can we believe them or not? Did God create the earth in seven literal days? Was there really a snake in the garden? Try not to let questions such as these distract you from the spiritual truths that the early chapters of Genesis were written to get across.

As the *Catechism of the Catholic Church* confirms, "The account of the fall in *Genesis* 3 uses figurative language, but affirms a primeval event, a deed that took place *at the beginning of the history of man.* (Cf. *Gaudium et Spes* 13 No. 1)" (No. 390). In other words, the stories at the start of Genesis are not literal, historical fact as we know it. Nonetheless, they do convey spiritual truth that is based in something that really did happen. These inspired chapters were never intended as a scientific or historic record but to help us understand important things about ourselves, our relationship to God, the problem of sin, and so on. They "express in their solemn language the truths of creation – its origin and its end in God, its order and goodness, the vocation of man, and finally the drama of sin and the hope of salvation" (No. 289).

These truths are the types of things that you want to be aware of as you read through Genesis. If you can keep that in mind, it may help keep you from getting stuck on some of the passages that sound strange or are hard to understand.

After you read about Creation and the Fall, look to see what the effects of the Fall are on Adam and Eve and their children and future generations. Notice also how God responds to wickedness in the world.

Remember that a very humble goal has been set for this trip through the Bible. All that is needed is an overview of the story as a whole (remember the "underpainting" described in the introduction?). Questions like "What happened here?" and "How was the story advanced?" or "Who is following God, and who is not?" are the kinds of things to be asking as you read. Later on, you can remember the *Early World* by the color turquoise, which represents the color of the Earth seen from space.

There will be questions and comments throughout the journal pages to help you focus on the big picture, and space to write your own questions so you can return to them later.

DAY
1

Date_____

Genesis ☐ 1      ☐ 2      ☐ 3      ☐ 4

*Adam and Eve's sin was transmitted to humanity in the form of a fallen nature: we are born lacking supernatural life in our souls. "Original sin" is not something we do, it is something we are: it is a state of being. Our souls are wounded. Our wills are weakened. We are subject to pain and death. We are inclined to sin. Thank God He had a plan to redeem us.*

*Soak in the poetry of Gen 1-2.*
*What does it tell you about God and creation?*

*What choice was given to Adam and Eve? Why did they fall?*

*What promise from God can be found in 3:15?*

*How do the effects of the Fall show up in the next generation?*
*In yours?*

?

_____

_____

_____

_____

_____

_____

_____

_____

_____

*Read John 1:1-14 to see how John uses the original creation story to shed light on a new one.*

_____

_____

_____

_____

_____

_____

## PRAYER

In the *Early World*, you created the heavens and Earth and tested Adam and Eve in the garden:

Help us to always choose the life that you offer.

**DAY 2**

Date_____

Genesis ☐ 5     ☐ 6     ☐7     ☐ 8

*Read 1 Peter 3:18-22 to learn the ultimate significance of the flood as it relates to life in Christ.*

JOURNAL

2

*Look for differences in the pattern used in Chapter 5 to describe each new generation. Who stands out and why?*

*Notice creation imagery and parallels to Genesis 1-2 in the flood story. Why would the author use these?*

*Noah "walked with God" (6:9) in a wicked generation. What can we learn from his example?*

**?**

_____

_____

_____

_____

_____

_____

_____

_____

_____

*What are those "nephilim" in chapter 6? And did people really live to be 900 years old?! Park these questions above so you can come back to them later.*

_____

_____

_____

_____

_____

_____

## PRAYER

In the *Early World*, you created the heavens and Earth and tested Adam and Eve in the garden:

Help us to always choose the life that you offer.

**DAY 3**

Date_____

Genesis ☐ 9     ☐ 10     ☐ 11

_Read the genealogies in Genesis 10 closely for clues to which family line will follow God. The details will help you identify the "good guys" and "bad guys" as you continue reading._

What's new in God's covenant with
Noah (ch 9) compared with Genesis 2?

Why were the people scattered at Babel?

What spiritual reality does that scattering illustrate?

This is the close of the Early World. What kind of a world is it?
What have you learned?

?

## PRAYER

In the *Early World*, you created the heavens and Earth and tested Adam and Eve
in the garden:

Help us to always choose the life that you offer.

# PATRIARCHS

## *Burgundy*

"Now the LORD said to Abram, 'Go from your country and your kindred and your father's house to the land that I will show you. And I will make of you a great nation, and I will bless you, and make your name great, so that you will be a blessing. I will bless those who bless you, and him who curses you I will curse; and by you all the families of the earth shall bless themselves" (Gen. 12:1-3).

# INTRODUCTION *to the* PATRIARCHS

◆　◇　◆　◆　◆　◆　◆　◆　◆　◆　◆　◆

**Narrative book:** Genesis 12 - 50

**Color:** Burgundy / God's blood covenant with Abraham

**Key people and events**

- God calls Abram out of Ur                          Gen. 12:1
- God's Covenant with Abraham:
  3-fold promise                                     Gen. 12
  - 1st covenant (land) Gen. 15
  - 2nd covenant (royal dynasty) Gen. 17
  - 3rd covenant (worldwide blessing)  Gen. 22
- The binding of Isaac                               Gen. 22
- Jacob wrestles with God,
  name changed to *Israel*                           Gen. 32:22-31
- Joseph sold into slavery                           Gen. 37:12-36
- Jacob's family moves to Egypt                      Gen. 46

As the world became inhabited, two types of civilization grew up: some people called on God's name and worshiped Him while others were violent and wicked, choosing self over God. God destroyed the wicked in a flood, sparing only the righteous Noah and his family, but the results of the Fall continued to echo through the generations. By Genesis 11 people had banded together to provide strength and security. They sought self-sufficiency, power, and a name for themselves through building a tower to heaven. God confused their languages and the *Early World* closed with mankind scattered in confusion.

We pick up the story in Genesis 12 many generations later, around 2,000 BC in Mesopotamia—the territory in and around the Tigris and Euphrates Rivers and their tributaries. It is the Middle Bronze Age. Rival city-states have been united under the kings of Ur. The culture is polytheistic. It is from this ancient civilization that God will take one of the descendants of Noah's son Shem, a man named Abram, calling him to leave everything and travel to a new place where He will make of him a nation, a new kind of civilization that will call on God's name.

The rest of Genesis tells the story of the *Patriarchs* (forefathers) of Israel—Abraham, Isaac, and Jacob—and also Jacob's son Joseph. As you read, focus on the promises God makes with Abraham and then renews with the others. In essence, that promise has three parts: God will give Abraham many descendants and the land of Canaan to live in; He will build from them a royal nation (kingdom); and they will be the source of blessing to the entire world. These promises form the basis of a *covenant*—a solemn oath that establishes a family bond—between God and Abraham's descendants, the nation of Israel. This covenant forms the blueprint for the rest of the Bible and is crucial to understanding it. It is a blood covenant, and the burgundy of that blood gives us a color by which to remember this period.

**DAY 4**

Date_____

Genesis ❏ 12　　❏ 13　　❏ 14　　❏ 15　　❏ 16

_Watch carefully what happens in chapters 12, 15, 17, and 22. Because of Abraham's obedience, a giant step will be taken toward the solution of the original problem: the broken relationship between God and mankind that occurred at the Fall._

*Look for evidence of Abraham's faith in chapters 12 and 15.*
*(Abraham is called "Abram" until chapter 17.)*

*What does God promise Abram? What else does He tell him?*

*In spite of God's promise, Abram and Sarai have no children.*
*How do they cope with that situation?*

**?**

_____

_____

_____

_____

_____

_____

_____

_____

_____

*Melchizedek (Gen. 14:18) means "king of righteousness;" Salem means "peace." The author of the Hebrews refers back to this priest/king to explain how Jesus has become the "surety" (or guarantee) "of a better covenant" than the one God made with Abraham. (Hebrews 7:11-22)*

_____

_____

_____

_____

_____

## PRAYER

In the time of the *Patriarchs*, you called Abraham and promised his children land, a royal kingdom, and worldwide blessing:

Help us always to hope in your promises.

## DAY 5

Date_____

Genesis ☐ 17  ☐ 18  ☐ 19  ☐ 20

*Gen. 19: Ancient rules of hospitality obliged Lot to protect his guests, even to the point of giving up members of his own family in their place.*

*Read Colossians 2:11-12 to see how the Old Covenant sign of circumcision is replaced by a sacrament: something that puts that which it signifies into effect.*

**5**

*What very important things happen in chapter 17?*

*How does God plan to keep His promise to "multiply"*
*Abraham "exceedingly" (17:2)?*

*Notice in chapter 18 the reason God says He chose Abraham.*

*For what has God chosen you?*

?

*Do the parallel stories in Genesis 12 and 20 confuse or trouble you? You're not alone.*
*Write down your questions above so you can return to them after you get the big picture.*

## PRAYER

In the time of the *Patriarchs*, you called Abraham and promised his children
land, a royal kingdom, and worldwide blessing:

Help us always to hope in your promises.

**DAY**

**6**

Date_____

Genesis ☐ 21    ☐ 22    ☐ 23    ☐ 24

*In Eden, Adam and Eve lost God's friendship. But James wrote that Abraham, who acted on what he believed, "was called the* friend of God" *(James 2:23). This model of faith can truly be called the father of all who believe. This is our story, not just the story of Israel. God's plan to restore His family does not build on blood-relationship but on the ties of faith.*

*Do you see any steps toward the fulfillment of God's promises?*

*How is Abraham required to prove, by his action, his trust in God?*

*Read chapter 22 with care.*
*How does Abraham's act foreshadow what God will ultimately do?*

*Think of all the things people trust God for in these chapters.*
*Can you trust God?*

**6**

JOURNAL

?

*Notice the paradox: It was only by giving up his son that Abraham became the father of the nation that would bless the world.*

## PRAYER

In the time of the *Patriarchs*, you called Abraham and promised his children land, a royal kingdom, and worldwide blessing:

Help us always to hope in your promises.

DAY
**7**

Date_____

Genesis ☐ 25   ☐ 26   ☐ 27   ☐ 28

*Ancient inheritance laws gave special rights to the first-born son, who received a double portion of the inheritance and took over as head of the family on his father's death. This birthright generally came also with a blessing; in our story this blessing carries with it God's covenant promises.*

*Notice how the blessing passes down to Isaac's descendants, and to whom.*

*What does chapter 25 tell you about Isaac and Rebekah's children, even before the boys are born? How does this play out as the story goes on?*

*What happens to Esau?*

*What vow does Jacob make after his dream of the heavenly stairway?*

**7**

J O U R N A L

**?**

## PRAYER

In the time of the *Patriarchs*, you called Abraham and promised his children land, a royal kingdom, and worldwide blessing:

Help us always to hope in your promises.

DAY

# 8

**Date**_____

**Genesis** ☐ 29    ☐ 30    ☐ 31    ☐ 32

---

*From now on, "Jacob" (deceiver or he grasps) will also be known as "Israel" (he struggles with God). The one who grasped with his own power for birthright and blessing had learned to struggle with God and be blessed. The nation that bears his name will exhibit the characteristics of both of these names.*

*How does Jacob get back what he dished out to his brother Esau?*

*Notice the names and number of Jacob's sons. These will be heads of the future tribes of Israel. Who is the firstborn?*

*What progress is made toward the fulfillment of God's promises?*

*Notice how Jacob gets a new name and what it means.*

8

## PRAYER

In the time of the *Patriarchs*, you called Abraham and promised his children land, a royal kingdom, and worldwide blessing:

Help us always to hope in your promises.

## DAY 9

Date_____

Genesis ☐ 33    ☐ 34    ☐ 35    ☐ 36

_Esau is the father of the Edomites, who settle south-southeast of the Dead Sea. They will later be enemies of Israel._

*The events of Genesis 34 are a shocking interlude in the story. Notice who is responsible; they will reap the consequences later on.*

*Jacob and his family return to Bethel in chapter 35. What happens there?*

*By listing Esau's descendants in chapter 36, the author in effect lays that branch of the family tree aside before following the line of Jacob.*

**?**

## PRAYER

In the time of the *Patriarchs*, you called Abraham and promised his children land, a royal kingdom, and worldwide blessing:

Help us always to hope in your promises.

**DAY**
**10**

Date_____

**Genesis** ☐ 37    ☐ 38    ☐ 39    ☐ 40

*"The account of Jacob"* that begins in Gen. 37 focuses not on Jacob's firstborn son, but on the oldest son of his favorite wife Rachel.

Watch the role that dreams play in the story of Joseph.

Chapter 38 interrupts with a contrasting account of Joseph's older brother Judah. What is he like? How is he different from Joseph? These two men will play key roles in the history of Israel.

**10**

JOURNAL

**?**

## PRAYER

In the time of the *Patriarchs*, you called Abraham and promised his children land, a royal kingdom, and worldwide blessing:

Help us always to hope in your promises.

## DAY 11

Date_____

Genesis ☐ 41      ☐ 42      ☐ 43      ☐ 44      ☐ 45

_Joseph is often seen as a "forerunner" of Jesus. These two beloved sons of their fathers are both betrayed and sold for silver. . .wrongly accused. . .and brought out from captivity/ death to life and glory; they both reconcile their brethren to their father. . .and become the source of food and life._

*How do Joseph's boyhood dreams (chapter 37) finally come to pass?*

*Do you see any change in Judah's character by the end of Gen. 44?*

*Watch how Joseph reconciles his brothers to his father.*

*Joseph might have despaired in the pit or in the prison, yet God used those things to raise him up and save others. How does that encourage you?*

**?**

## PRAYER

In the time of the *Patriarchs*, you called Abraham and promised his children land, a royal kingdom, and worldwide blessing:

Help us always to hope in your promises.

## DAY 12

Date_____

Genesis ☐ 46   ☐ 47   ☐ 48   ☐ 49   ☐ 50

*Jesus will one day be born into the tribe of Judah. The "scepter" Jacob speaks of in 48:8-10 points forward to the universal kingship that will belong one day to him who is also known as the "lion of the tribe of Judah," the Messiah.*

*Genesis 48-49 record Jacob's final blessing on his 12 sons and, by extension, upon the tribes that will descend from them. They are blessed in birth-order; read to see why the first three lose the rights of the first-born (remember Simeon and Levi from Gen. 34?).*

*The death of Joseph marks the close of the Early World. What kind of a world is it? What have you learned?*

**12**

JOURNAL

**?**

_____
_____
_____
_____
_____
_____
_____
_____
_____

Key verse: Genesis 50:20

_____
_____
_____
_____
_____

## PRAYER

In the time of the *Patriarchs*, you called Abraham and promised his children land, a royal kingdom, and worldwide blessing:

Help us always to hope in your promises.

*"Sing to the LORD, for he has triumphed gloriously; the horse and his rider he has thrown into the sea" (Ex. 15:21).*

# INTRODUCTION *to* EGYPT *and* EXODUS

◆  ◆  ◇  ◆  ◆  ◆  ◆  ◆  ◆  ◆  ◆  ◆

**Narrative book:** Exodus

**Color:** Red / the Red Sea

**Key people and events**

| | |
|---|---|
| • Slavery in Egypt | Ex. 1 |
| • Moses and the burning bush | Ex. 3 |
| • The ten plagues on Egypt | Ex. 7-11 |
| • Exodus / the First Passover (1280 BC) | Ex. 12-14 |
| • The Crossing of the Red Sea | Ex. 13-15 |
| • Manna from heaven | Ex. 16 |
| • God's covenant with Moses (Mt. Sinai) | Ex. 19-31 |
| • The sin of the golden calf | Ex. 32 |
| • The Tabernacle | Ex. 25-27, 36-38 |
| • The Levitical priesthood | Ex. 32:27-29; Num. 3 |
| • 12 spies sent out | Num. 13 |

The next historical period, *Egypt and Exodus*, is told in the book of Exodus. Before you read, take stock of what you know so far. This is not an isolated story, it is connected in very important ways to the events of Genesis. There are two things in particular that it will be helpful to notice.

First, recall that the focus of the *Patriarchs* was on God's promise to Abraham: to give him many descendants and a nation in the land of Canaan; to build from them a royal kingdom; and finally to make them a blessing to the entire world.  The opening words of Exodus will show how God is beginning to make good on that promise:  Abraham's grandson Jacob brought his family to Egypt and there they have prospered and multiplied to the point where the new Pharaoh, 400 years later, is threatened by their presence.  They may be slaves at the start of this period, but God has promised to make of them a nation.  Watch how He does it.

Second, think back to the very beginning and remember that God created mankind in His image and that He rested on the seventh day.  Part of being created in God's image means that people were created for this rhythm of work and rest, and in their rest they lift their hearts to worship and acknowledge their Creator.  Now what might you expect to happen, if God's people are kept from living in His image?  That is the crux of the conflict presented in Exodus.  Who will the people serve and work for, and in whose image will they live?

Exodus 1-18 tells how God liberates His people from Egyptian bondage.  The Red Sea crossing gives us the color (red) for the period of *Egypt and Exodus.*  In chapters 19-40, Israel spends a year at the foot of Mt. Sinai, learning basic lessons in how to live as the people of God and preparing to enter the Promised Land.  A new covenant forms them as a nation.  They are given laws to live by and have God's presence in their midst (in the Tabernacle) for the first time since the Garden of Eden.  This book is full of lessons for us today.  For now, though, try to get the outline of the story and the overarching themes.  The Exodus will become the defining event in Israel's history and it will be referred back to many times in the rest of the Bible.

**DAY 13**

Date_____

Exodus  ☐ 1     ☐ 2     ☐ 3     ☐ 4

*YHWH comes from the Hebrew verb "to be" and means I AM. It has no tense and encompasses all tenses. When you read the word Lord (in capital letters) in your English translation, it refers to this name.*

This is the first time God has revealed His name and therefore His character. What does it tell you about God?

What is the purpose of the signs God gives Moses to use in chapter 4?

"Let my son go (halak) that he may serve (obed) me," says God in 4:23. "Go (halak) now, and work (obed)," replies Pharaoh (5:18). Who is this battle between? What are the stakes?

?

In the Gospels, we see how Jesus lives out the life of Israel. Matthew highlights several incidents that echo these chapters in Exodus, including the Holy Family's sojourn in Egypt and the murder of the innocent young boys.

## PRAYER

You freed your people from slavery in Egypt so they could worship you:

Free us from sin so we can serve and worship.

DAY
14

Date_____

Exodus  ☐ 5     ☐ 6     ☐ 7     ☐ 8

*Jesus applied "I AM" to himself in his teaching, thereby claiming to be God (John 6:35; 8:12; 9:5; 10:7, 9, 11, 14; 11:25; 14:6; and 15:1-5).*

*Pay attention to the reasons Pharaoh refuses to let Israel go.*

*What does Moses ask of Pharaoh in chapter 5?*

*Underline all the "I ams" and "I wills" in chapter 6 and notice how they amplify the meaning of I AM.*

*When you read about the plagues in chapters 7-8, keep in mind that Egypt worshiped the Nile (as the source and sustainer of life) and various gods that took the form of animals.*

**14**

JOURNAL

?

## PRAYER

You freed your people from slavery in Egypt so they could worship you:

Free us from sin so we can serve and worship.

DAY
15

Date_____

Exodus  ☐ 9     ☐ 10     ☐ 11     ☐ 12

_Israel was to "keep this service" (observe this rite) of the Passover as a lasting ordinance. The word translated "service" is the same word used in chapter 1 for slavery. It is worth pondering how service to God differs from service to Pharaoh._

From 9:29, what is the purpose of the plagues?

The plague of darkness comes without warning and does not affect the land of Goshen. What would this mean to a nation that worshiped the sun god, Ra, and whose Pharaoh was believed to be its embodiment on earth?

The seven-day Feast of Unleavened Bread begins with the Passover meal. Leaven (yeast) is a symbol of sin or wickedness.

**15** JOURNAL

**?**

We show our "service" to God through the liturgy (lit. "the work of the people"). We eat bread and drink wine as a memorial of Christ's sacrifice just as at Passover, Jews eat lamb as a memorial of the Passover sacrifice.

## PRAYER

You freed your people from slavery in Egypt so they could worship you:

Free us from sin so we can serve and worship.

DAY
16

Date_____

Exodus   ☐ 13     ☐ 14     ☐ 15     ☐ 16

Read John 6 to discover the
relationship between the manna
of Exodus and the "bread from
heaven" in the New Testament,
and think about how what
you've read about manna helps
your understanding of Jesus'
words.

*Pay attention to 14:12-14. What part did Israel play in their own deliverance?*

*Freed from Egypt, Israel needs to learn to live as God's people. They are like little children who must learn to rely on Him for all their needs. When you read about the ways they are tested and the way God provides, consider what lessons they are meant to learn. How do those lessons speak to you?*

**16**

JOURNAL

**?**

## PRAYER

You freed your people from slavery in Egypt so they could worship you:

Free us from sin so we can serve and worship.

# DAY 17

**Date**_____

**Exodus**  ☐ 17    ☐ 18    ☐ 19    ☐ 20

*If the question in Exodus 1–18 was **"Who will you serve?"** then the question starting in chapter 19 might be **"How will you serve?"** Israel spends a year at the base of Mt. Sinai after leaving Egypt. During that time they meet God, they hear His voice, and they become His people.*

*How does Moses' father-in-law help him handle his heavy load?*

*What kind of nation does God say Israel will be, if they obey Him and keep His covenant? (19:1-6)*

*The terms of that covenant (the things God requires of Israel in return) can be found in Exodus 20. These are commands that liberate. They tell Israel how to live as redeemed people, to keep from falling back into bondage. They can do the same for us.*

**17**

?

_____

_____

_____

_____

_____

_____

_____

_____

_____

*Israel must learn that if they put God first in their lives, He will watch over them. Read Luke 12:16-31 to see how this concept is preserved in the New Covenant.*

_____

_____

_____

_____

_____

## PRAYER

You freed your people from slavery in Egypt so they could worship you:

Free us from sin so we can serve and worship.

DAY
18

Date_____

Exodus ☐ 21   ☐ 22   ☐ 23   ☐ 24

*Notice the way Israel enters a covenant with God in chapter 24; the law they have just received is in effect the terms Israel agrees to. This is a binding agreement that establishes them as God's people.*

Exodus 21-23 is "the Book of the Covenant" — a list of ordinances that apply the basic laws found in the Ten Commandments to everyday situations that Israel will face as a nation. Chapter 23 emphasizes the importance of worshiping God alone, keeping prescribed feasts, and obeying and serving God. Try not to linger too long in these chapters, but save a closer look for later study.

What comfort and warnings does God give at the end of chapter 23?

**18**

JOURNAL

?

## PRAYER

You freed your people from slavery in Egypt so they could worship you:

Free us from sin so we can serve and worship.

## DAY 19

*The Ark held symbols of the Messiah to come: manna (bread from heaven), the Ten Commandments (the Word), Aaron's rod (symbol of high-priestly authority). It foreshadows the day when God will come to earth and live among his people as a man, Immanuel ("God with us").*

*Try to read quickly through the instructions in these four chapters. Rather than getting every detail, list the things they were asked to build and their purpose, if you know it.*

*What is the purpose of the Tabernacle? What kind of materials will be used, and how will they be obtained?*

*Focus on the Ark of the Covenant and its contents. This will be the earthly throne of God, who is coming to dwell among His people.*

**?**

## PRAYER

You freed your people from slavery in Egypt so they could worship you:

Free us from sin so we can serve and worship.

DAY
20

Date_____

Exodus    ☐ 29    ☐ 30    ☐ 31    ☐ 32

Chapter 32 marks the start of
the "Levitical priesthood," when
members of the tribe of Levi are
set apart to the Lord as priests
in place of the first-born of each
family, who previously filled
that function.

*Who in particular are named in chapter 29 as the priests?*

*What strikes you most about the instructions to priests? Jot down any questions for later study.*

*Notice the importance given to the Sabbath observance in chapter 31.*

*The incident of the Golden Calf is a turning point in the drama. Pay attention to the way God deals with infidelity and to the way Moses intercedes for the people.*

**20**

**?**

## PRAYER

You freed your people from slavery in Egypt so they could worship you:

Free us from sin so we can serve and worship.

DAY
21

Date_____

Exodus ☐ 33  ☐ 34  ☐ 35  ☐ 36

Continue to watch the way that Moses intercedes with God on behalf
of His people and reunites them when the people disobey.
On what basis does he appeal for God's mercy?

What things are revealed to Moses about God and
His nature in chapter 34?

Notice the outpouring of gifts and talent when
work on the Tabernacle has begun.

**21**

JOURNAL

?

The importance of keeping the Sabbath is stressed immediately after instructions for work are
given and again right before the work begins. In light of what you have already read:
Why is a day of rest so important to the Lord? How does this speak to you?

## PRAYER

You freed your people from slavery in Egypt so they could worship you:

Free us from sin so we can serve and worship.

**DAY**
**22**

Date_____

Exodus   ☐ 37      ☐ 38      ☐ 39      ☐ 40

*These chapters may seem repetitious.*
*Read through and note their general message.*

*Notice the theme of completion of work, its quality ("as the Lord commanded") and consequent blessing that runs through these chapters. Does it echo the creation of anything else?*

*On what note does Exodus end?*
*How would you characterize this period?*

**?**

## PRAYER

You freed your people from slavery in Egypt so they could worship you:

Free us from sin so we can serve and worship.

# DESERT WANDERINGS

*Tan*

*"According to the number of the days in which you spied out the land, forty days, for every day a year, you shall bear your iniquity, forty years, and you shall know my displeasure" (Num. 14:34).*

# INTRODUCTION *to* DESERT WANDERINGS

◆  ◆  ◆  ◇  ◆  ◆  ◆  ◆  ◆  ◆  ◆  ◆

**Narrative book:** Numbers

**Color:** Tan / the color of the desert sand

**Key people and events**

- 12 Spies sent out ................................ Num 13
- Aaron's budded rod ............................ Num. 17
- Moses strikes the rock ........................ Num. 20
- The bronze serpent ............................ Num. 21:4-9
- Covenant in Moab .............................. Deut. 29

The book of Exodus chronicled the most significant event in the formation of the people of Israel: their dramatic deliverance by God from Egyptian slavery. In their early days of freedom, God provided His new family with all that they needed: protection; food from heaven; water from a rock. He gave them strong leaders and established them with a new covenant as a nation. He gave them the Law, which was essentially instructions for how to live as free children of God. He gave them the Levitical priesthood to help them approach Him and worship. And He gave them the Tabernacle: a place where He could meet with them and a tangible sign of His dwelling in their midst.

Getting Israel out of Egypt and setting them up as His people was one thing. It soon became evident that the real trick would be purging Egypt from their hearts. They are children still, spiritually, and they need to learn to trust their Father and walk in faith before they are ready to possess the land that was promised them. The book of Numbers picks up the story here and tells how they fare in the period of *Desert Wanderings*.

Numbers gets its English name from the census God has them take at the start of the book and again at the end, when they prepare to finally enter the land of Canaan. The book's title in Hebrew (*bemidbar*) means "in the desert"—which is closer to the name of this period. Numbers describes the 40-year period that Israel spends wandering in the desert on the way to Canaan from Mt. Sinai. This time of wandering is God's judgment on Israel for their complaining, lack of faith, and refusal to trust Him to give them the land that He promised them. As a result, the generation that had seen God's deliverance from Egypt will lose their share in the land. Only after that generation dies in the desert will their children see the God's promise fulfilled.

DAY
23

Date_____

Numbers  ☐ 1      ☐ 2      ☐ 3      ☐ 4

_____
_____
_____
_____
_____
_____
_____
_____
_____
_____
_____
_____
_____
_____
_____

*The tribe of Levi was not counted in the census because they had no military role and would not be fighting. God set them apart after the golden calf incident to care for the Tabernacle. Notice their position in chapter 2 in relationship to the tabernacle and to the other tribes, which are being put into a formal marching order.*

_____
_____
_____
_____
_____
_____
_____
_____

*Rather than concentrating on the details in chapters 1 & 2, just note the basics. What's being done and why?*

*In chapters 3 and 4, hone in on the responsibilities of the Levites and of the various clans.*

*The tabernacle provided a way for the people to approach God. What do all these careful instructions say about Him?*

?

*The 12 tribes of Israel are descended from the 12 sons of Jacob (aka Israel). After removing Levi, the total number of 12 tribes was maintained by counting Joseph as two tribes under his sons Ephraim and Manasseh.*

## PRAYER

You taught Israel to walk in faith through 40 years' wandering in the desert:

Help us to trust in you, O God.

**DAY 24**

Date _____

Numbers ☐ 5   ☐ 6   ☒ 7   ☒ 8

⑦ The Nazirites -
     cut hair, nodrink - spend time w God.
• The priestly Benidict. 6:22-27 pg 189
Deut - ⑥ - law Hear Israel, The Lord Our
God is our God - warning + remembering
Bought out Egypt - slave God done for you
rules commands - relationship w God
a Blessing - my The word of Lord be in Mind, Mouth, Heart

God chosen us

⑧ The 7 lamps
     - Levites' Consecration + Services
⑨ Passover kept a Sinai
     The cloud + The Fire
⑩ on The Move - from Sinai
         Deuto
         ch 8: a warning not to forget God
         ch 9 consequences Rebelling against
         God warning

*You are bound to have questions regarding the details of particular customs. Don't let them sidetrack you from seeing the big picture! Jot down the really troublesome things to go back to later.*

JOURNAL

**24**

Chapter 5 looks at obvious aspects of uncleanness and also at those that are hidden, like wronging another person or being unfaithful to a spouse. The instructions in the latter case are meant to keep others from making unfounded accusations.

The Aaronic benediction in 6:22-26 is a well-loved blessing you may be familiar with. It speaks of the peace and blessing that come only from the Lord, and which can be yours in spite of your circumstances.

?

Read 2 Corinthians 6:14-18. What parallels do you see with the instructions in Numbers 6, that apply to us today?

## PRAYER

You taught Israel to walk in faith through 40 years' wandering in the desert:

Help us to trust in you, O God.

Date_____

Numbers  ☑ 9      ☐ 10      ☑ 11      ☐ 12

11 - Complaining in the Desert
   The Seventy Elders.
   The quails.

12 - Aaron + Miriam - speak against Moses
     Miriam is punish - Unit for emmy God
13 - Spies Sent to Cannon - negitive report
     saw more powerful groups -

*The Ark of the Covenant leads the people as they go out as a conquering army. This is an ongoing reminder that God is establishing this kingdom, and it is His power—not theirs—that will determine the victory.*

*This is the first time Israel will have celebrated the Passover since they left Egypt.*

*How was God's presence made visible to Israel?*

*God continued to provide for His people in the desert. How did they respond, and what was the result?*

*Did you notice what chapter 12 says about Moses?*

JOURNAL

25

**?**

## PRAYER

You taught Israel to walk in faith through 40 years' wandering in the desert:

Help us to trust in you, O God.

DAY
26

Date_____

Numbers ☐ 13    ☐ 14    ☐ 15    ☐ 16

The Levites (the tribe of Levi) alone stood up for the Lord after the golden calf incident. As a result, God set them apart in place of the first-born of the nation to serve him. Among the Levites, Aaron and his sons were given the priesthood. Korah is a Levite who wants to be a priest. The other challengers are from the tribe of Reuben.

*Chapters 13-14 are key chapters in Numbers. Is Israel ready to conquer Canaan? Why or why not?*

*How does the punishment for Israel's lack of faith and rebellion "suit the crime"?*

*God's response to Korah's rebellion might seem harsh. What does it tell you about God's prerogative to appoint leaders? About the sanctity of those "set apart"? When Korah and co. challenge Moses, who are they really challenging?*

**26** JOURNAL

## PRAYER

You taught Israel to walk in faith through 40 years' wandering in the desert:

Help us to trust in you, O God.

DAY
**27**

Date_____

Numbers ☐ 17    ☐ 18    ☐ 19    ☐ 20

*Aaron's budded rod (his staff) will be kept along with the stone tablets of the Ten Commandments and a jar of manna in the Ark of the Covenant as a permanent witness.*

*How does God tell Israel who He has chosen to be their spiritual leader and high priest (chs. 17–18)? Why do you think He uses such dramatic means?*

*Chapter 20 occurs back at Kadesh, where the people were sent off on their wanderings after quarrelling and rebelling. This time their lack of faith drives Moses to sin—with what result?*

*"Edom" (20:14–21) descends from Jacob's brother Esau.*

**27**

JOURNAL

**?**

## PRAYER

You taught Israel to walk in faith through 40 years' wandering in the desert:

Help us to trust in you, O God.

**DAY 28**

Date_____

Numbers ☐ 21    ☐ 22    ☐ 23    ☐ 24

*The Plains of Moab are just east of the Jordan River across from Jericho. God has led Israel in a number of military victories and the local kings are nervous. Why do they hire Balaam?*

*Why can't Balaam do as the kings want? Notice the magnitude of blessing he pronounces on Israel in chapters 22-24.*

*What does it say to you, that God blesses so abundantly people who continue to grumble and have trouble trusting Him?*

**?**

*The bronze snake was a "type" of something to come. Read John 3:14 and ponder it in light of Exodus 21.*

## PRAYER

You taught Israel to walk in faith through 40 years' wandering in the desert:

Help us to trust in you, O God.

DAY
**29**

Date_____

Numbers ☐ 25   ☐ 26   ☐ 27   ☐ 28

*The animals Israel was to sacrifice were animals revered by the surrounding nations. It has been suggested that one reason for all the animal sacrifices was to help free Israel from the tendency to idol worship that had taken hold of them in Egypt and that would be a continual temptation to them in Canaan.*

Israel's sin with the Baal of Peor leads to a special role for the descendants of Phinehas. Many years later, during the period of the Royal Kingdom, his descendant Zadok will be a faithful high priest under King David.

Do you remember the purpose of the census in Numbers 1? Why is another one being taken now?

Pay attention to the person designated to succeed Moses and what he will be appointed to do.

**29** JOURNAL

## PRAYER

You taught Israel to walk in faith through 40 years' wandering in the desert:

Help us to trust in you, O God.

**DAY**
**30**

Date_____

Numbers ☐ 29    ☐ 30    ☐ 31    ☐ 32

*The tribes of Reuben and Gad, along with half of Manasseh, were given land in the "Transjordan": an area to the east of the Jordan River and extending roughly from the middle of the Salt Sea in the South to Mt. Hermon in the North. They left their families there while the men continued across the Jordan to help conquer Canaan.*

God declares a holy war in chapter 31 against Midian for seducing Israel to worship the Baal of Peor and engage in sexual immorality. Balaam, the prophet who prophecied blessing on Israel, is killed for his role in instigating the affair.

From chapter 32—who among those who came out of Egypt were granted passage into the Promised Land, and why?

**?**

Three feasts are announced in Numbers 29. The first will later become Rosh Hashanah, a celebration of the new year. The "holy convocation" described next is the "Day of Atonement" or Yom Kippur, an annual day set aside to atone for sins. Finally comes the "Feast of Tabernacles" (Hebrew Sukkot), a joyful festival commemorating the 40 years of wandering and the harvest. "Tabernacles" refers not to the Tabernacle God had them build but to the temporary booths the people lived in during that time.

## PRAYER

You taught Israel to walk in faith through 40 years' wandering in the desert:

Help us to trust in you, O God.

## DAY 31

Date_____

Numbers ☐ 33    ☐ 34    ☐ 35    ☐ 36

The "Year of Jubilee" (36:4): According to Mosaic law, every 50th year was to be a "jubilee year" in which people return home, slaves are set free, debts remitted, and land returned to original owners.

Pay particular attention to the warning at the close of chapter 33.

After tribal boundaries are outlined in chapter 34, notice the two types of towns that are set apart in chapter 35 and their respective purposes.

The Desert Wanderings are over. How would you characterize this period?

**31**

JOURNAL

?

## PRAYER

You taught Israel to walk in faith through 40 years' wandering in the desert:

Help us to trust in you, O God.

# CONQUEST and JUDGES

*Green*

◆

*"Thus the LORD gave to Israel all the land which he swore to give to their fathers; and having taken possession of it, they settled there" (Josh. 21:43).*

*"And all that generation also were gathered to their fathers; and there arose another generation after them, who did not know the LORD or the work which he had done for Israel. . . . Then the LORD raised up judges, who saved them out of the power of those who plundered them" (Jgs. 2:10, 16).*

# INTRODUCTION *to* CONQUEST *and* JUDGES

◆   ◆   ◆   ◆   ◇   ◆   ◆   ◆   ◆   ◆   ◆   ◆

**Narrative book:** Joshua, Judges, 1 Samuel 1 - 8

**Color:** Green / the green hills of Canaan

**Key people and events**

| | |
|---|---|
| • Israel crosses the Jordan | Josh. 1-4 |
| • The fall of Jericho | Josh. 5:13-6:27 |
| • Covenant renewal under Joshua | Josh. 8:30-35 |
| • Southern campaign | Josh. 9-10 |
| • Northern campaign | Josh. 11 |
| • Tribal allotment | Josh. 13-21 |
| • Israel asks Samuel for a king | 1 Sam. 8 |

*Desert Wanderings* chronicled the 40 years Israel spent wandering after they failed to trust God to take them victoriously into the Promised Land. Remember it by the color tan for the sands of the desert. It stands in sharp contrast to the triumphant red of deliverance for *Egypt and Exodus* and the lush green of the hills of Canaan—the setting for our next period, *Conquest and Judges.*

Before moving on, it is worthwhile to note these words of Moses as he renewed God's covenant with the people shortly before his death (this can be found in the supplemental book for this time period, Deuteronomy): *"Hear, O Israel: the LORD our God is one LORD; and you shall love the LORD your God with all your heart, and with all your soul, and with all your might. And these words which I command you this day shall be upon your heart; and you shall teach them diligently to your children. . .. Take heed lest you forget the LORD, who brought you out of the land of Egypt, out of the house of bondage. You shall not go after other gods, of the gods of the peoples who are round about you. . .. And you shall do what is right and good in the sight of the*

*LORD, that it may go well with you, and that you may go in and take possession of the good land which the LORD swore to give to your fathers"* (Deut. 6:4-7, 12, 14, 18).

Will they remember? Will they go after other gods? And will they teach their children? You will find out as you read. In the book of Joshua, Moses' successor leads the conquest of the Promised Land. The rest of this period is told in the book of Judges and a few chapters of I Samuel. Before Joshua dies, he reminds the people that God is with them and will continue to be so, if only they will love and obey Him. God freed them from Pharaoh so they could serve Him; now it will be up to them to choose Yahweh over the gods of the Canaanites. Judges shows how they live up to this challenge. As you read you will follow a cycle in which Israel sins; falls into servitude; turns to God in supplication; experiences salvation at the hand of a God-sent judge; and then falls into a period of silence before the cycle begins again. By the end of the period they will be fed up and will ask God to give them a king.

**What about all the violence?**

A word before you begin reading: many people find the violence in these stories tough to swallow. How could a loving God demand such wholesale slaughter? This is not easy to answer. As you read, try to put these books in the perspective of the story as a whole. Why is there violence and death in the world to begin with? What is God doing, by raising up this new nation to call on His name instead of exalting its own? What have we seen is the result of people turning from God, so far in the story? What happens to everyone when a community compromises and allows sin to grow unchecked? Think of how a truly just and holy God should deal with those who persist in their sin vs. how He should deal with those who repent. The Canaanites were known not just for idol worship but for their violence and immorality. They have been warned, but they do not repent. God is punishing idolatrous nations who obstinately follow their own ways.

Most importantly, though, let the Bible answer the questions for you as you read. You will notice that the tribes that settle South of Jerusalem (primarily Judah) obey God and wipe out the Canaanites. In the North, they don't. What is the result? By the time you read the last few chapters of Judges, you may feel differently than you did at the start of Joshua. It is hard for holiness to flourish when it compromises with corruption. We should know that from our own lives.

**DAY 32**

Date_____

Joshua ☐ 1 ☐ 2 ☐ 3 ☐ 4

*The Jordan River, which is usually 10-20 feet wide, can be a mile wide during the spring flood stage—which it was at the time of their crossing (3:15). If God used natural means to cut off the flow of the river at Adam, the timing is nonetheless miraculous.*

*What will be the key to Joshua's success?*

*How does this "spy mission" differ from the one in Numbers 13?*

*Why was Rahab eager to help Israel?*

*What dramatic sign does God give Israel to reassure them of His presence and might (chapter 3)? (And think about it: what would it say to a people who worshiped a water god?)*

## 32

JOURNAL

**?**

*Look for spiritual parallels in Ephesians 6:11–18 to God's message to Joshua in chapter 1.*

## PRAYER

You led Israel triumphantly into the Promised Land. They failed to teach their children, and instead did what was right in their own eyes:

Help us to keep our eyes on you and bring up our children in your way.

*Why was Achan's theft such a big deal? These first cities and everything in them were to be "devoted to the Lord" (6:17)—almost as the first-fruits of a harvest belong to God—but by destruction. Achan was not stealing just any plunder, he was stealing what belonged to God and at the outset of their mission. This sin would affect the entire nation and it was punished accordingly.*

*Notice the two very important ceremonies that are resumed before Israel proceeds with the conquest.*

*With what "weapons" are the walls of Jericho destroyed?*

*Israel's conquest of Canaan foreshadows the spiritual conquest of the world by Christ and His Church. What does it teach about the importance of cleansing our hearts from sin, and what happens when we hang onto things that should be done away with?*

**33**

JOURNAL

?

_____
_____
_____
_____
_____
_____
_____
_____
_____
_____

*2 Corinthians 10:3-4 speaks of the nature of the war we are carrying on today and the weapons God gives us to destroy the enemy. Think about them in light of the fall of Jericho.*

_____
_____
_____
_____
_____
_____

## PRAYER

You led Israel triumphantly into the Promised Land. They failed to teach their children, and instead did what was right in their own eyes:

Help us to keep our eyes on you and bring up our children in your way.

DAY
34

Date_____

Joshua    ☐ 9    ☐ 10    ☐ 11    ☐ 12

*It is not known what exactly happened when "the sun stood still, and the moon stayed" (10:13). What is clear is that God intervened on Israel's behalf and brought them victory.*

*Gibeon's deceit may have saved their lives,
but what were the consequences?*

*By thoroughly defeating Jericho, Ai, and other cities in the central
region, Joshua has driven a wedge among rival kingdoms before they
can band together against him. He now takes on kingdoms in the
north and south separately (Numbers 10-12).*

**34**

JOURNAL

## PRAYER

You led Israel triumphantly into the Promised Land. They failed to teach
their children, and instead did what was right in their own eyes:

Help us to keep our eyes on you and bring up our children in your way.

DAY
35

Date_____

Joshua    ❏ 13    ❏ 14    ❏ 15    ❏ 16

*The Canaanites attributed power over things like life, water, fertility, etc. to a number of gods.  Once the Israelites settle there, they will be tempted to attribute prosperity to those gods as well.  It is crucial that they remember what Yahweh has done for them so they can stay faithful.*

*Joshua 13–21 tells how the land is divided among the remaining tribes (remember that some have received land in the Transjordan).*

*At the start of chapter 13, not all the land has been taken. Notice what God says about it.*

*You may want to skim through these chapters, but notice the extent to which the local people are driven out or destroyed.*

**35**

JOURNAL

**?**

## PRAYER

You led Israel triumphantly into the Promised Land. They failed to teach their children, and instead did what was right in their own eyes:

Help us to keep our eyes on you and bring up our children in your way.

DAY
36

Date_____

Joshua    ☐ 17    ☐ 18    ☐ 19    ☐ 20

Joseph and Judah are the two sons who received real blessing from their father Jacob (see Journal Day 12). The "house of Joseph" is literally the tribes of his sons, Ephraim and Manasseh, which take up the bulk of the northern territory. The entire northern area is often later called Ephraim. Judah is the main tribe to the south. Notice in chapter 19 that Simeon receives its portion within Judah. Benjamin lies horizontally between Judah and Ephraim.

*Pay attention to Joshua 18:5; it will have importance as the story goes on.*

*If your Bible contains maps, take time to study a map showing how the 12 tribes were arranged, noting the key cities.*

*In the ancient world, murder often led to an endless series of revenge killings. How was Israel to safeguard against this?*

**36**

JOURNAL

?

*"The avenger of blood" (20:3) is also known as the "kinsman-redeemer." His job as closest relative was to avenge murder but also to redeem from slavery or marry a widow and give her a son to carry on the dead man's name. Boaz is a kinsman-redeemer in the book of Ruth.*

## PRAYER

You led Israel triumphantly into the Promised Land. They failed to teach their children, and instead did what was right in their own eyes:

Help us to keep our eyes on you and bring up our children in your way.

# DAY 37

Date_____

Joshua  ☐ 21  ☐ 22  ☐ 23  ☐ 24

*Israel was up against formidable strongholds as they sought to enter and settle in the Promised Land. What spiritual strongholds do you face as you seek to "enter the rest" of God's Kingdom? What can you learn from their struggle?*

*The Levites were not given a block of land but were spread in cities among the other tribes. Why do you think this was so?*

*Notice how the end of chapter 21 wraps up this section.*

*What warning did Joshua give the eastern tribes before blessing them and sending them on their way? (chapter 22)*

*Joshua 23-24 gives Joshua's farewell address. What is his warning to the leaders? (chapter 23)*

**37** JOURNAL

?

*"As for me and my house, we will serve the LORD" (24:15)*

## PRAYER

You led Israel triumphantly into the Promised Land. They failed to teach their children, and instead did what was right in their own eyes:

Help us to keep our eyes on you and bring up our children in your way.

**DAY**
**38**

Date_____

Judges  ☐ 1    ☐ 2    ☐ 3    ☐ 4

*A seven-fold cycle of sin and deliverance is detailed in 3:7 — 16:31. This cycle was described in the Introduction to this period. Notice its phrases as you read.*

*Chapters 1:1 — 3:6 give a kind of prologue to the book of Judges, showing first how Israel fought the remaining inhabitants of the land and then how they fared in keeping the covenant.*

*Keep in mind the territorial divisions described on Day 36 as you read. Compare and contrast the way the north and the south occupy their respective territories, as there will be ramifications later on.*

*Pay close attention to 2:6-23 and record what you learn.*

**38**

JOURNAL

?

## PRAYER

You led Israel triumphantly into the Promised Land. They failed to teach their children, and instead did what was right in their own eyes:

Help us to keep our eyes on you and bring up our children in your way.

# DAY 39

Date_____

Judges ☐ 5 ☐ 6 ☐ 7 ☐ 8

*Throughout Judges, notice the influence of the pagan nations and false gods upon Israel (these nations are people and gods Israel allowed to remain in the land that they conquered).*

*Gideon and his son Abimelech form the central account in the repeating cycle (chs. 6-9). Together they represent the best and the worst among leaders.*

*What do chapters 6 and 7 tell you about the ways of God in "impossible" situations?*

*What is Gideon's response to the people's request that he rule over them (8:22-23)?*

**39** JOURNAL

?

_____

*Psalm 115 contrasts the God of Israel with the false gods of the nations around them.*

_____

## PRAYER

You led Israel triumphantly into the Promised Land. They failed to teach their children, and instead did what was right in their own eyes:

Help us to keep our eyes on you and bring up our children in your way.

Date _____

Judges    ☐ 9      ☐ 10      ☐ 11      ☐ 12

*How does Abimilech rule differently than Gideon did? What is the result?*

*The heartbreaking story of Jephthah and his daughter (chapter 11) illustrates the binding nature of vows in the ancient world.*

*Don't worry about getting all the details of these stories. Focus on the main strokes: is Israel faithful? What draws her away from God? What / who keeps her from being absorbed into the Canaanite culture? and so on.*

**40**

JOURNAL

**?**

## PRAYER

You led Israel triumphantly into the Promised Land. They failed to teach their children, and instead did what was right in their own eyes:

Help us to keep our eyes on you and bring up our children in your way.

## DAY 41

Date_____

Judges ☐ 13 ☐ 14 ☐ 15 ☐ 16

*"Nazirite" means "separated" or "dedicated." Those who made a vow of separation to God as a Nazirite abstained from alcohol and left their hair uncut as a sign of their vow. Their consecration was one of total devotion to God and sometimes lasted a lifetime.*

*The lone hero Samson is a picture of Israel during the time of the Judges: consecrated to God, given a unique role and God-given strength, yet flirting with (and even marrying!) the enemy. Blindness and slavery are the result.*

*What was the ultimate source of Samson's strength?*

*What is the ultimate source of your strength?*

## PRAYER

You led Israel triumphantly into the Promised Land. They failed to teach their children, and instead did what was right in their own eyes:

Help us to keep our eyes on you and bring up our children in your way.

DAY
42

Date_____

Judges ☐ 17 ☐ 18 ☐ 19 ☐ 20 ☐ 21

_The book of Ruth was written during this time and is a welcome counterpoint to the closing chapters of Judges: a Moabite woman forsakes the gods of Moab to faithfully serve Yahweh. Ruth appears in the genealogy of Jesus. She is in many ways what Israel was called to be._

The rest of Judges forms an epilogue that describes two incidents that most likely took place toward the start of the period. Write down the phrase that flanks this section (17:6 and 21:25).

At the time of the events of chapter 20, the high priest and the Ark of the Covenant were at Bethel, a town in the north of the tribe of Benjamin.

Did going their own way lead to freedom for Israel, or to something else? What is the cost of doing "what is right in your own eyes"?

**42**

JOURNAL

?

## PRAYER

You led Israel triumphantly into the Promised Land. They failed to teach their children, and instead did what was right in their own eyes:

Help us to keep our eyes on you and bring up our children in your way.

DAY
43

Date _____

I Samuel ☐ 1    ☐ 2    ☐ 3    ☐ 4

Hannah's prayer of thanksgiving has been called the "Magnificat of the Old Testament." Ultimately its anticipation of an anointed king (the Messiah) finds its fulfillment in the birth of another "impossible child" to the woman Mary.

*his is not the first time we have read about a child given to someone who was previously barren. Pay attention: this child will become the last and the greatest of all the judges.*

*Do you see proofs of God's initiative and purpose for Samuel in the details of Samuel's early life?*

*Contrast the first and last verses of chapter 3.*

**43**

JOURNAL

**?**

## PRAYER

You led Israel triumphantly into the Promised Land. They failed to teach their children, and instead did what was right in their own eyes:

Help us to keep our eyes on you and bring up our children in your way.

DAY
44

Date_____

1 Samuel  ☐ 5        ☐ 6        ☐ 7        ☐ 8

_____
_____
_____
_____
_____
_____
_____
_____
_____
_____
_____
_____
_____
_____
_____
_____
_____
_____
_____
_____
_____
_____
_____
_____
_____

*This marks the close of
Conquest and Judges.  How
would you summarize this
period?*

*Ask yourself why God delivered Israel to the Philistines and allowed the Ark to be taken. What is different between this situation and their first foray into battle in the Promised Land, when God had them march against Jericho led by the Ark?*

*It is the end of the era of the judges, and the people ask for a king. Why do they want one, and what does this show about their relationship with the Lord? Notice what God tells Samuel will be the outcome of their request for a king, and their response.*

**44**

JOURNAL

## PRAYER

You led Israel triumphantly into the Promised Land. They failed to teach their children, and instead did what was right in their own eyes:

Help us to keep our eyes on you and bring up our children in your way.

# ROYAL KINGDOM

*Purple*

"...I will make for you a great name, like the name of the great ones of the earth ... Moreover the LORD declares to you that the LORD will make you a house. When your days are fulfilled and you lie down with your fathers, I will raise up your offspring after you, who shall come forth from your body, and I will establish his kingdom. He shall build a house for my name, and I will establish the throne of his kingdom for ever" (2 Sam. 7:9, 11-13).

# INTRODUCTION *to the* ROYAL KINGDOM

◆   ◆   ◆   ◆   ◆   ◇   ◆   ◆   ◆   ◆   ◆   ◆

**Narrative book:** 1 Samuel 9 – 30; 2 Samuel; 1 Kings 1 - 11

**Color:** Purple / royalty

**Key people and events**

| | |
|---|---|
| • Saul chosen king | 1 Sam. 9 |
| • David anointed by Samuel | 1 Sam. 16 |
| • David king of Israel | 2 Sam. 5 |
| • David moves Ark to Jerusalem | 2 Sam. 6 |
| • God's covenant with David | 2 Sam. 7 |
| • Solomon proclaimed king | 1 Kgs. 1 |
| • Solomon builds first Temple (961 BC) | 1 Kgs. 5-8 |

In the preceding period, Israel entered and occupied the promised land of Canaan but failed to drive out the Canaanites. The book of Judges shows in living color what happened when Israel chose its way over God's way. They did not teach their children what they had learned. Every man did what was right in his own eyes. They married the Canaanites, they worshiped like them, they became like them. The horrors narrated in the final chapters paint a vivid picture of just how far they fell.

Watching the moral deterioration that resulted when Israel disobeyed God's command to completely drive out the Canaanites puts that command into perspective. Yes, God was punishing those nations for their wickedness. He was also teaching Israel a lesson. They could not exist as His people if they continued to "straddle the fence" and flirt with idolatry. Their apostasy with the Golden Calf and with the Baal of Peor made it clear that a radical cutting-away of temptation would be needed if Israel was indeed to become a blessing to the other nations and lead the way to God.

Unfortunately, as we have seen, Israel did not completely obey and they reaped the fruit of their disobedience. The book of Judges does have its high points, its examples of faith and of God's faithfulness to His children. But the rollercoaster of sin, supplication, and salvation leaves us wondering: just what will it take to break the cycle? And where is the kingdom God promised? Other than the 12 judges, there has been no real leader over Israel for nearly 200 years. By the first chapters of I Samuel, the people have had enough and demand a king so they can be like the other nations. The next period is *Royal Kingdom*, which is told in the rest of I Samuel, in 2 Samuel and in part of I Kings. This is the long-awaited time in which God establishes Israel as One Holy Kingdom. God will give Israel what they asked for, and in the process, He will give them (ultimately) what they need and what He means them to have: His kingship. The people may be fickle, but God never forgets His promises.

You will read about many people in these chapters. Focus on the three kings who reign in this high point of Israel's history, each for approximately 40 years:

- Saul, a tall, handsome hero from the tribe of Benjamin, unites the 12 tribes of Israel into a kingdom but ultimately loses the kingdom when he fails to trust God.

- David, from the line of Judah, is a "man after God's own heart" who expands the kingdom and to whom God promises an eternal throne.

- David's son Solomon builds a permanent Temple in Jerusalem. He is known for his great wisdom, but even that doesn't protect him from sin or its consequences.

The key chapter to focus on in this period is 2 Samuel 7, in which God establishes a covenant with King David that expands upon His second promise to Abraham, the promise of royal kingdom and dynasty. That promise reaches a preliminary fulfillment in the earthly kingdom of Israel, a kingdom that pre-figures the eternal kingdom of God.

Date_____

1 Samuel ☐ 9    ☐ 10    ☐ 11    ☐ 12

*What kind of a man is Saul?*

*Notice what is said in 1 Samuel 10:6, 10:10, and 11:6.*

*The "rights and duties of the kingship" mentioned in 10:25 were written in a legal document that would have distinguished Israel's king from the kings of other nations and clarified his role in relation to the ongoing lordship of Yahweh.*

**45**

*What is the gist of Samuel's farewell speech to Israel in chapter 12?*

?

## PRAYER

You established a kingdom on your servant David and promised him an eternal throne:

Establish your kingdom in our midst.

**DAY 46**

Date_____

1 Samuel ☐ 13 ☐ 14 ☐ 15 ☐ 16

*When God rejects Saul as king, He doesn't depose him immediately. Saul will continue as king until his death, but there will be no ongoing dynasty based on him and his sons.*

*Saul's offense in chapter 13 is not light. His authority as king was not to be absolute, but subject to the word of God. By disregarding Samuel's instructions, he was disobeying God.*

*Do the events in chapter 14 reveal Saul to be a man "after the Lord's heart" or a king "like all the nations" have?*

*Saul's second major offense is recorded in chapter 15. Notice what his punishment reveals about God, as explained by Samuel in verses 22-23.*

**?**

*Read John 1:1-14 to see how John uses the original creation story to shed light on a new one.*

## PRAYER

You established a kingdom on your servant David and promised him an eternal throne:

Establish your kingdom in our midst.

## DAY
## 47

Date_____

1 Samuel ☐ 17    ☐ 18    ☐ 19    ☐ 20

*Don't skip through the story of David and Goliath just because it is familiar. What does it tell you about God?*

*Saul's jealousy of David will continue to grow through the years. In what ways are his attempts to kill David thwarted?*

*Notice the strength of the relationship between David and Saul's son Jonathan and the covenant made between them.*

47

JOURNAL

**?**

## PRAYER

You established a kingdom on your servant David and promised him an eternal throne:

Establish your kingdom in our midst.

DAY
48

Date_____

1 Samuel ☐ 21    ☐ 22    ☐ 23    ☐ 24

The "holy bread" or "bread of the Presence" in chapter 21 was an offering of thanks placed daily before the Lord in the Holy Place in the Tabernacle. It was meant to be eaten only by the priests, but Ahimelech makes a compassionate decision to feed David's men.

Compare and contrast the actions of David and King Saul in these chapters.

Why does David spare Saul when he has the opportunity to kill him?

**?**

Read Matthew 12:3-4 to see how Jesus uses 1 Samuel 21 in his teaching regarding the Sabbath laws.

## PRAYER

You established a kingdom on your servant David and promised him an eternal throne:

Establish your kingdom in our midst.

**DAY 49**

Date_____

1 Samuel ☐ 25  ☐ 26  ☐ 27  ☐ 28

*Divination and sorcery were prohibited by Mosaic law, and Saul himself had put the mediums and wizards out of the land.*

In chapter 27, David takes refuge among the Philistines. He continued to conduct raids against Israel's enemies (people who the Israelites failed to defeat during the conquest) while allowing Achish to believe he was making raids on Israel.

Setting aside questions of what exactly happened in Saul's encounter with the witch at Endor, what very clear message was sent to Saul at that time?

**49**

JOURNAL

?

## PRAYER

You established a kingdom on your servant David and promised him an eternal throne:

Establish your kingdom in our midst.

**DAY**
**50**

Date_____

1 Samuel ☐ 29    ☐ 30    ☐ 31

*Accepting refuge from Achish meant that David and his men were obligated to provide military service to him. The skepticism of the other Philistine commanders saved David from being forced to play his bluff and fight Israel.*

*Where did David find strength to face the bitter situation they found at Ziklag in chapter 30?*

*How can you find similar strength in difficult situations?*

**50**

JOURNAL

## PRAYER

You established a kingdom on your servant David and promised him an eternal throne:

Establish your kingdom in our midst.

DAY
51

Date_____

2 Samuel ☐ 1     ☐ 2     ☐ 3     ☐ 4

*The lame man Mephibosheth (chapter 4), son of David's dear friend Jonathan, is the only remaining heir in Saul's line after the murder of Ish-bosheth.*

*The book of 2 Samuel describes David's kingship and the Covenant God makes with him.*

*What is David's response to the deaths of Saul and Jonathan?*

*In chapter 2, David becomes king over "the house of Judah"—the southern part of the kingdom,—while "the house of Saul" (under Saul's commander Abner) establishes Saul's son Ish-bosheth as king over the northern territories. The resulting civil war lasts more than 7 years.*

**51**

JOURNAL

?

## PRAYER

You established a kingdom on your servant David and promised him an eternal throne:

Establish your kingdom in our midst.

**DAY**
**52**

Date_____

**2 Samuel** ☐ 5    ☐ 6    ☐ 7    ☐ 8

*A dynasty is marked by a succession of kings in the same family. It is sometimes known as a "house," as in England's House of Windsor.*

*What does David accomplish in his first years as King over all of Israel?*

*As you read about the Ark of the Covenant, ask what the incidents in the first half of chapter 6 teach about the Lord's presence and rule.*

*When the Lord gives David rest from his enemies, he wants to build a permanent dwelling place for the Ark. What is God's reply?*

*What kind of king is David shown to be in chapter 8?*

**52**

JOURNAL

?

## PRAYER

You established a kingdom on your servant David and promised him an eternal throne:

Establish your kingdom in our midst.

DAY
# 53

Date_____

2 Samuel ☐ 9    ☐ 10    ☐ 11    ☐ 12

*How does David make good on the promise he made to Jonathan years earlier (cf. 1 Samuel 20)?*

*Notice the Lord's love for David's son Solomon from the start (12:25).*

*Psalm 51 records David's prayer for forgiveness after his sin with Bathsheba. Read and meditate on it if you have time.*

**53**

JOURNAL

?

## PRAYER

You established a kingdom on your servant David and promised him an eternal throne:

Establish your kingdom in our midst.

**DAY**
**54**

Date_____

2 Samuel ❐ 13    ❐ 14    ❐ 15    ❐ 16

*When Absolom goes "in to his father's concubines in the sight of all Israel," he is directly challenging David and making a play for his throne.*

54

*David's sin with Bathsheba and Uriah has major repercussions (chs. 11–20) but God is true to His promise and will not take the kingdom from him. As you read, consider why this is true, when Saul lost the kingdom for disobedience.*

*How does David's failure to forgive Absalom worsen the situation between them?*

**?**

## PRAYER

You established a kingdom on your servant David and promised him an eternal throne:

Establish your kingdom in our midst.

**DAY 55**

Date_____

2 Samuel ☐ 17    ☐ 18    ☐ 19    ☐ 20

*How does God intervene on David's behalf? (17:14)*

*Notice David's love for Absalom in spite of his treachery.*

*Seeking to be restored to the throne after Absolom's death, David appeals to his home tribe of Judah. Notice the reaction among those from the other (Northern) tribes (19:43 – 20:2).*

**55**

JOURNAL

?

## PRAYER

You established a kingdom on your servant David and promised him an eternal throne:

Establish your kingdom in our midst.

**DAY**
**56**

Date_____

2 Samuel ☐ 21    ☐ 22    ☐ 23    ☐ 24

*How do David's "last words" (23:1–7) describe the righteous king?*

*Twice before, we have seen a census taken of Israel's military men: both were in preparation for the conquest of Canaan. The census in chapter 24 appears to have been taken by David out of pride or glory in his own might. Consider what David's reactions during the ensuing punishment reveal about David's character and about God.*

**?**

*Chapter 22 is a great song of praise by David that is also recorded in Psalm 18. In it he magnifies God for His steadfast love toward the anointed king of Israel.*

## PRAYER

You established a kingdom on your servant David and promised him an eternal throne:

Establish your kingdom in our midst.

## DAY 57

Date_____

1 Kings   ☐ 1      ☐ 2      ☐ 3      ☐ 4

*King Solomon wrote thousands of proverbs, many of which are preserved in the book of Proverbs. Read chapters 1 and 2 for some of his insights into the importance of wisdom.*

*The third king of Israel is Solomon, David's son by Bathsheba. What kind of man is he?*

*Pay attention to the charge David gives Solomon before he dies.*

*Bathsheba sits on a throne at the king's right hand. Her position of Queen Mother foreshadows the position of Mary, Mother of Jesus and Queen of heaven, who intercedes on our behalf with her son.*

**57**

JOURNAL

## PRAYER

You established a kingdom on your servant David and promised him an eternal throne:

Establish your kingdom in our midst.

DAY
58

Date_____

1 Kings ☐ 5 ☐ 6 ☐ 7 ☐ 8

*Read 1 Corinthians 3:16 to discover what the Jerusalem Temple prefigures in the New Covenant.*

*What does Solomon do, that David was denied?*

*What was signified by the cloud that fill the temple of the Lord on its completion? (cf. 8:11-12)*

*Now that there exists a physical, permanent structure to house the presence of God in Jerusalem, will the Lord be bound to remain there? What is at the heart of Solomon's prayer in chapter 8?*

## PRAYER

You established a kingdom on your servant David and promised him an eternal throne:

Establish your kingdom in our midst.

DAY
59

Date_____

1 Kings  ☐ 9    ☐ 10    ☐ 11

This marks the close of the Royal Kingdom. How much of God's original promise to Abraham has been fulfilled? What aspects of it remain?

Don't miss God's promise to Solomon at the start of chapter 9, and the conditions attached.

According to Moses, Israel's king was not to multiply horses, wives, or large amounts of silver and gold for himself. Does Solomon follow this command? What is the result?

Pay particular attention to 11:26-43. What prophecy is given to Jeroboam, and what hope is given for the long-term outlook of David's dynasty and the kingdom?

**?**

_____
_____
_____
_____
_____
_____
_____
_____
_____
_____

_____
_____
_____
_____
_____

## PRAYER

You established a kingdom on your servant David and promised him an eternal throne:

Establish your kingdom in our midst.

# DIVIDED KINGDOM

*Black*

◆

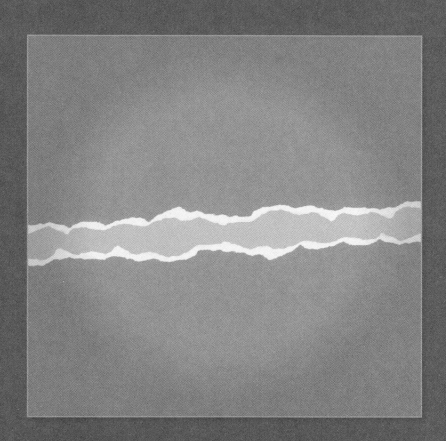

*"And when all Israel heard that Jerobo'am had returned, they sent and called him to the assembly and made him king over all Israel. There was none that followed the house of David, but the tribe of Judah only" (1 Ki. 12:20).*

# INTRODUCTION *to the* DIVIDED KINGDOM

❖ ❖ ❖ ❖ ❖ ❖ ◇ ❖ ❖ ❖ ❖ ❖

**Narrative book:**  1 Kings 12-22; 2 Kings 12-17 (Israel);
2 Kings 12-25 (Judah)

**Color:**  Black / Israel's darkest period

**Key people and events:**

- The Kingdom divides into
  Israel (N) and Judah (S)                1 Kgs. 12:16-20
- Kings of Israel and Judah
  until Northern Exile                    1 Kgs. 12 – 2 Kgs 17
- The ministries of Elijah and Elisha
  and other prophets                      1 Kgs. 17 – 2 Kgs. 8
- Judah from Hezekiah to the
  Babylonian Captivity                    2 Kgs. 18 – 25

During the period of the *Royal Kingdom*, Saul united the kingdom of Israel under a single ruler, then David expanded it and Solomon built it up.  At the height of its glory, Israel must have looked like a near-final fulfillment of God's promises to Abraham:  they possessed most of the strategic land of Canaan and were in a position to bless the surrounding nations.  God dwelt among them in a magnificent temple in Jerusalem.  Their king was the wisest and wealthiest man on earth.  The nation was blessed and the people prospered.  Most of all, God had promised to establish David's throne—and his line through Solomon— forever.  What could go wrong?

What indeed. At the close of that period, God promised to tear away the bulk of the kingdom from Solomon's son because of Solomon's sin. The resulting split will launch Israel into the period of the *Divided Kingdom*. The first few chapters you read will frame the entire period: The ten tribes to the North will rebel against Solomon's son and reject his rule over them. The result will be two separate kingdoms. The one to the South is called Judah; it is ruled over by kings in David's line from the royal city of Jerusalem. The one to the North, called Israel, is ruled over by a succession of dynasties from its capital, Samaria. Elsewhere in the world, the balance of power will shift from Egypt to Assyria around 900 BC. Take note when you see Assyria mentioned; it and successive powers to the north of Canaan will have a dramatic impact on the future history of God's people.

You will notice that after describing the division itself, the narrative jumps back and forth between Israel and Judah so that some sense of chronology is maintained. The account is organized according to the reigns of the many kings. Each time you read that someone new is on the throne, pay attention to whether the king is of Judah (South – David's line – Jerusalem) or Israel (North – various dynasties – Samaria). It may help you to have a *Bible Timeline* chart available as reference. Don't worry about remembering all the details. This first time through it is enough to get the flavor of what is going on in each of the kingdoms. Do they follow God, or not? What is the result?

The *Divided Kingdom* period is represented by the color black because it is Israel's darkest hour. The story is told in I Kings 12-22 and in 2 Kings, which are the narrative books for the period.

# DAY 60

Date_____

1 Kings   ☐ 12   ☐ 13   ☐ 14   ☐ 15

_In spite of the evil done by kings of Judah, God promises to maintain a "lamp" for David in Jerusalem forever. This symbolizes the permanence of the Davidic dynasty in the city where God has chosen His name to dwell._

*Solomon's son Rehoboam may reign over just one tribe, but he is still heir to the throne of David and God's presence still dwells in the Jerusalem temple, which is located in Judah.*

*What dilemma does the location of Jerusalem pose for Jeroboam? How does he solve it and with what result?*

*The reigns of the first eight kings of the Northern Kingdom (Israel) are described in 1 Kings 15:25 — 16:34 and chapter 21.*

**?**

*During the time of the Divided Kingdom, the territory north of Jerusalem continues to be called Israel. The territory to the south remains loyal to David's throne and is called Judah.*

## PRAYER

Israel split into rival kingdoms and fell into idolatry:

Help us to choose your kingship over other loves.

**DAY**
**61**

**Date**_____

**1 Kings**  □ 16   □ 17   □ 18   □ 19

*A succession of nine dynasties ruled the Northern kingdom. Most were ended by bloodshed.*

A long succession of kings follows Jeroboam in the Northern kingdom of Israel. What refrain appears nearly verbatim in the account of each king? (The first is in 15:34)

List the kings of Israel described in these chapters. What kind of men are they? What is Israel like during this time?

God sent prophets to carry His messages of warning and love to Israel. One of the greatest was Elijah (chs. 17-19). What is God's message to Israel through Elijah?

**61**

JOURNAL

?

## PRAYER

Israel split into rival kingdoms and fell into idolatry:

Help us to choose your kingship over other loves.

DAY
62

Date_____

1 Kings ☐ 20 ☐ 21 ☐ 22

In chapter 20, notice the reason God delivers the army of Ben-Hadad into Ahab's hands.

Ahab can't confiscate Naboth's land (chapter 21) because the land belongs to God, who granted each family a permanent inheritance that was to be preserved.

Jehoshaphat (22:41-50) is a king of Judah; his account is sandwiched between Ahab and Ahab's son Ahaziah, both kings of Israel.

**62** JOURNAL

?

*On what note does 1 Kings end?*

## PRAYER

Israel split into rival kingdoms and fell into idolatry:

Help us to choose your kingship over other loves.

DAY
63

Date_____

2 Kings ☐ 1 ☐ 2 ☐ 3 ☐ 4

**63**

*2 Kings picks up where 1 Kings left off, with God's judgment on Ahab's son Ahaziah through the prophet Elijah.*

*Elijah's mantle—and a double portion of his spirit—falls (literally!) on Elisha when the older prophet is taken up to heaven in the whirlwind.*

*How do the miracles Elisha does in Israel show God's grace and His desire to bless those who follow Him?*

**?**

*Elijah will appear years later with Moses on the Mount of Transfiguration, where they speak to Jesus. Together they represent the law (Moses) and the prophets (Elijah).*

## PRAYER

Israel split into rival kingdoms and fell into idolatry:

Help us to choose your kingship over other loves.

DAY
64

**Date**_____

**2 Kings**  ☐ 5  ☐ 6  ☐ 7  ☐ 8

*"The LORD has called for a famine...for seven years" (8:1): famine is a covenant curse due to Israel's unfaithfulness to her covenant with God.*

In chapter 5, notice how each person stands in relationship to God (the king of Israel; the Israelite servant girl; the king of Aram; Namaan the Aramean).

After 66 years of good kings and finally peace, the evil king Jehoram takes the throne in Judah (chapter 8). How might his choice of a wife (Athaliah, daughter of Ahab) have affected his reign?

## PRAYER

Israel split into rival kingdoms and fell into idolatry:

Help us to choose your kingship over other loves.

**DAY 65**

Date_____

2 Kings ☐ 9   ☐ 10   ☐ 11   ☐ 12

*God will ultimately punish the people of the Kingdom of Israel for their apostasy by removing them from the Promised Land. Watch in chapter 10 as God begins to reduce the size of their territory.*

*Jehu is anointed king of Israel and is appointed to destroy the house of Ahab.*

*Notice how the relationship to Ahab's family proves deadly in chapters 11–12.*

*How is the line of David saved?*

**65** JOURNAL

?

*Young king Joash is a bright light in the history of Judah.*

## PRAYER

Israel split into rival kingdoms and fell into idolatry:

Help us to choose your kingship over other loves.

DAY
66

Date_____

2 Kings    ☐ 13     ☐ 14     ☐ 15     ☐ 16

_2 Kings 16 brings the narrative right up to the fall of the northern kingdom. Judah will hold on a while longer before falling itself. Those stories are told in the next period, Exile._

*Under Jeroboam II, Israel's northern borders are secured and Israel enjoys a respite from foreign pressure. The people become complacent, worship other gods and fail to follow God's commands. God sends the prophets Amos and Hosea to announce that God will punish them with exile to Assyria—the new world power to the North.*

*The Assyrian invasions against Israel and Judah are ferocious, brutal, and devastating. They will bring Israel to its knees and weaken Judah.*

**66** JOURNAL

?

*Read Hosea 1-3 to hear how God tenderly calls Israel to return to their covenant relationship, even as He declares the consequences of their harlotry.*

## PRAYER

Israel split into rival kingdoms and fell into idolatry:

Help us to choose your kingship over other loves.

# EXILE

*Baby Blue*

"*The people of Israel walked in all the sins which Jerobo'am did; they did not depart from them, until the LORD removed Israel out of his sight, as he had spoken by all his servants the prophets. So Israel was exiled from their own land to Assyria until this day*" (2 Ki. 17:22-23).

"*So Judah went into captivity, away from her land*" (2 Ki 25:21).

# INTRODUCTION *to the* EXILE

❖ ❖ ❖ ❖ ❖ ❖ ❖ ◇ ❖ ❖ ❖ ❖

**Narrative book:** 2 Kings 17, 25

**Color:** Baby blue / Singing the blues in Baby-lon

**Key people and events:**

- Israel falls to Assyria (722 BC)               2 Kgs. 17
- Foreign possession of Samaria               2 Kgs. 17
- Judah falls to Babylon (587 BC)             2 Kgs. 25
- Babylon destroys the first Temple (587 BC)    2 Kgs. 25

By about 1050 BC Israel at last had her kingdom, but it quickly ran aground when Solomon turned his eyes from God and focused on building for himself. His son only made things worse, precipitating a drastic split. David's royal kingdom of Israel divided into two kingdoms: "Judah" (two tribes) in the south and "Israel" (ten tribes) in the north. Israel's king, Jeroboam, set up golden calves at two centers of worship to replace the Temple, appointed his own priests, and established new festivals. Under this alternate religion Israel quickly foundered. About 200 years followed of apostasy, violence, Baal worship, and the like. Despite repeated warnings from God's prophets, there was no change. By 722 BC the time for punishment had come. The period of Exile begins in the north when the people of Israel are conquered by Assyria and scattered abroad.

Judah fared somewhat better, with good kings periodically calling the people back to God. For about 350 years after Solomon, David's dynasty held the throne in Jerusalem. However, the people continued to fall into idol worship and failed to heed the prophets' warnings. Around the time that the Northern Kingdom fell, Isaiah foretold that Judah too would be punished with exile, this time to the new world power Babylon. This prophecy will come true starting with deportations in 605 and 597 BC and culminates in 587 BC when Judah falls to Babylon and Solomon's Temple is destroyed. It will be another 70 years before the people of Judah are allowed to return from their so-called "Babylonian captivity."

 The dark, black days of the Divided Kingdom now spill into the baby blue of the Exile (you can remember the color of this period by thinking of Judah "singing the blues" in "Baby-lon"). The reading for this period is short: just 2 Kings 17 (which tells of the fall and deportation of Israel) and 2 Kings 25 (which tells of the exile of Judah). The intervening chapters, which you will also read in this section, tell how Judah, in the South, fares after the conquest of the Northern Kingdom, Israel. Many of the prophets write during this time: Jeremiah and Ezekiel, Daniel and Baruch to name a few. After you finish this 90-day initial journey through the Bible, you may want to return and read some of the prophets in context. It will greatly enrich your understanding of the period—just as a basic familiarity with the period will help you better understand those books.

DAY
67

Date_____

2 Kings ☐ 17 ☐ 18 ☐ 19 ☐ 20

*During the Divided Kingdom, "Israel" refers to the north. After Israel is exiled, all that is left is what had been Judah— and the prophets start referring to the Southern Kingdom as Israel. The name has a connotation ("God's people") that is not confined to geographic boundaries.*

Chapter 17 tells how Israel is conquered by Assyria and exiled.
Verses 17-23 explain the reason why. Think about it: what
spiritual conditions does exile represent?

Meanwhile, back in Judah.... God had promised His people land,
abundant life, and blessing if they would only trust and follow
Him. In 18:28-35, consider how Sennacherib's "offer" to Judah
compares. (Sennacherib was the King of Assyria; he marched against
Jerusalem after deporting the Northern Kingdom).

**67**

JOURNAL

**?**

Read Isaiah 5-6 to see what happens when the people flout God's commands.

## PRAYER

You punished first Israel, then Judah, with exile. Prophets brought a message
of hope:

In our exile due to sin, show us the way home.

DAY
68

Date_____

2 Kings   ☐ 21   ☐ 22   ☐ 23   ☐ 24   ☐ 25

The messianic hopes of Israel include the belief that the 12 tribes of Israel will be fully restored under a Davidic king. In Romans 11, when Paul says "all Israel" will be saved, he means all 12 tribes—including the people of the diaspora, those from the North who were scattered.

Much of King Hezekiah's good was undone by his son Manasseh
(21:1-18).

2 Chronicles tells us that Manasseh was humbled near the end of
his reign and tore down the pagan altars and tried to make amends.
But it was too little, too late for Judah.

Take note of the eventual end of Judah and the cause of its demise.
What ray of hope can be found in the final verses of 2 Kings?

JOURNAL

68

**?**

Jeremiah 34 is a final warning to Judah under King Zedekiah. The prophet berates them for
failing to keep the Jubilee.

## PRAYER

You punished first Israel, then Judah, with exile. Prophets brought a message
of hope:

In our exile due to sin, show us the way home.

# RETURN

## *Yellow*

"Thus says Cyrus king of Persia: The LORD, the God of heaven, has
. . . charged me to build him a house at Jerusalem, which is in Judah.
Whoever is among you of all his people, . . . let him go up to Jerusalem,
which is in Judah, and rebuild the house of the LORD. . ." (Ez. 1:2,3).

# INTRODUCTION *to the* RETURN

◆　◆　◆　◆　◆　◆　◆　◆　◇　◆　◆　◆

**Narrative book:** Ezra, Nehemiah

**Color:** Yellow / Judah returns to brighter days

**Key people and events**

- Cyrus allows Judah to return        Ezra 1
- Zerubbabel rebuilds the Temple     Ezra 3-6
- Ezra returns and teaches (458 BC)   Ezra 7-8
- Nehemiah returns, rebuilds
  Jerusalem walls (444 BC)          Neh. 3-4

The state of the divided kingdom at the close of the period of Exile is as follows: Israel, the Northern Kingdom, was conquered by Assyria in 722 BC and the tribes that composed it ceased to exist in any meaningful way. Most of the people were deported and scattered. In their place, King Sargon imported people from five other conquered nations and settled them in the area of Samaria. These intermarried with the remaining Israelites. The mixed population of Samaritans that resulted worshiped the God of Israel right along with the gods they brought from their homelands. In 587 BC, the Southern Kingdom (Judah) fell to the Babylonians, who destroyed Jerusalem and the Temple and carried off many of the Judeans to exile in Babylon. God's faithfulness to His people and to the promises He made regarding David's throne—despite their infidelity—can be seen in the messages of the prophets of that time, who prophesied destruction and exile but also held out the hope of restoration and a new covenant. (The prophets are not included in this quick read through the story; read them later to get a fuller picture of the time periods of the Divided Kingdom and Exile.)

The next period, Return, will chronicle Judah's return home after 70 years of Babylonian exile. Remember it by the color yellow, representing brighter days. The people return in three waves over about a hundred years. The story is told in the narrative books of Ezra (who describes the first two returns) and Nehemiah. Before you read, try to imagine yourself into the scene. Knowing all that the Promised Land and the Kingdom meant to Israel, what must it have been like to be away from that land for so long? What damage has been done to the place and the people? What kind of healing is required to make them whole? Amid all the events that are described, focus on the three types of rebuilding that take place during this time of return: Zerubbabel will lead Judah in rebuilding the Temple; Ezra will rebuild their spiritual lives by teaching the law; and Nehemiah will head an effort to rebuild the Jerusalem walls.

Two new world powers come into play during this time and greatly influence the course of events: Persia, which gains ascendancy at the start of the period, and Greece, which follows about 200 years later. In secular history, this is the time of Plato, Socrates, and Aristotle.

**DAY 69**

**Date**_____

**Ezra** ☐ 1 ☐ 2 ☐ 3 ☐ 4 ☐ 5

*King Cyrus founded the Persian Empire by uniting the Medes and Persians. At his coronation he read a "charter of freedom" granting people freedom from slavery, freedom of religion, and freedom from oppression.*

God used an unlikely person to return His people to the Promised Land. How has He worked through unlikely people in your life?

Zerubbabel was a man in David's bloodline. What did he accomplish in the first return? (Ezra 3)

In chapters 4-6, notice the kind of opposition the people faced and how they were helped.

JOURNAL 69

?

Read the prophecy mentioned in 1:1 in Jeremiah 29:10-14. God gave the people hope from the outset of the Exile.

## PRAYER

You brought the exiles back to Canaan; they rebuilt the Temple and Jerusalem and were taught once more from your Law:

Rebuild our broken hearts and lives as we return to you.

Date _____

**Ezra**     ❏ 6      ❏ 7      ❏ 8      ❏ 9      ❏ 10

*Ezra descends from a high priestly line that went back to the days of David and Solomon. He is also a scribe, or teacher of the Law of Moses, who has devoted himself to studying and teaching God's word.*

*Ezra returns with the second wave of exiles (chapter 7). Why is he sent to Jerusalem? Notice the help that he receives.*

*In chapters 9-10, Ezra finds that in spite of God's mercy, some of the people have married foreign wives, one of the sins that got them into trouble to begin with. His solution may seem radical to us but is necessary for a new start. The people need to return to God wholeheartedly and follow Him alone.*

**?**

___

*The book of Esther, which fits between the first and second returns, gives us a window into the lives of those who chose to remain in Persia.*

___

## PRAYER

You brought the exiles back to Canaan; they rebuilt the Temple and Jerusalem and were taught once more from your Law:

Rebuild our broken hearts and lives as we return to you.

DAY
**71**

Date_____

Nehemiah ☐ 1    ☐ 2    ☐ 3    ☐ 4

*Malachi prophecies during the Return, calling the people to faithfulness and reverence and warning of the coming Day of the Lord.*

*The third wave of return from captivity is told in the book of Nehemiah.*

*Why does Nehemiah return? How does he fare?*

*Notice the source of opposition to rebuilding the walls of Jerusalem. Samaria's continued opposition—combined with their syncretistic religion—is the source of the friction we see in the New Testament between the Jews and the Samaritans.*

**71**

JOURNAL

?

## PRAYER

You brought the exiles back to Canaan; they rebuilt the Temple and Jerusalem and were taught once more from your Law:

Rebuild our broken hearts and lives as we return to you.

# DAY
# 72

Date_____

Nehemiah ☐ 5     ☐ 6     ☐ 7     ☐ 8

*What crisis does Nehemiah confront in chapter 5?*

*How does he solve it?*

*The Feast of the Tabernacles ("booths" or tents) described at the close of chapter 8 is a week-long feast held in remembrance of the 40 years the children of Israel spent dwelling in tents in the wilderness before entering Canaan.*

**72**

JOURNAL

?

## PRAYER

You brought the exiles back to Canaan; they rebuilt the Temple and Jerusalem and were taught once more from your Law:

Rebuild our broken hearts and lives as we return to you.

**DAY 73**

**Date** _____

**Nehemiah** ☐ 9  ☐ 10  ☐ 11  ☐ 12  ☐ 13

*Jerusalem is populated by volunteers and by people chosen by lot from among the priests and Levites, the gatekeepers, and the descendants of Judah and Benjamin (previous members of the kingdom of Judah). Most of the people preferred to stay in their home towns.*

*A corporate confession of sin and a recitation of God's dealings with Israel begins these readings. To what important act do they lead?*

*What final reforms are made by Nehemiah?*

*This is the end of the Return.
What kind of a new start has been made?*

**73**

?

## PRAYER

You brought the exiles back to Canaan; they rebuilt the Temple and Jerusalem and were taught once more from your Law:

Rebuild our broken hearts and lives as we return to you.

# MACCABEAN REVOLT

## Orange

"*And Mattathias and his friends went about and tore down the altars ... They rescued the law out of the hands of the Gentiles and kings, and they never let the sinner gain the upper hand*" (1 Macc. 2:45, 48).

# INTRODUCTION *to the* MACCABEAN REVOLT

❖ ❖ ❖ ❖ ❖ ❖ ❖ ❖ ❖ ◇ ❖ ❖

**Narrative book:** I Maccabees

**Color:** Orange / fire in the oil lamps in the purified Temple

**Key people and events:**

- Conquests of Alexander the Great     1 Macc. 1
- Persecutions of the Jews     1 Macc. 1
- Mattathias refuses pagan worship     1 Macc 2
- Antiochus desecrates the Temple
  (167 BC)     1 Macc. 4:43
- Purification of the Temple
  (Hanukkah – 164 BC)     1 Macc. 4:36-61

The Babylonian exile came to an end when Cyrus, King of Persia, came to power and freed the Judeans to return and rebuild the Temple. Those who made the journey south did so in three stages. Under the leadership of Zerubbabel, Ezra, and Nehemiah, they rebuilt the Temple and the Jerusalem walls and learned from God's Law. At the close of our reading, we saw the people confess their sins and make another covenant—a binding agreement—with the Lord.

After this "remnant" of Jews returned to the land, they lived in relative peace for a century and were quite faithful to the Covenant. Around 336 BC, Alexander the Great swept across Asia, conquering nations and extending the rule of a new power, Greece. He aimed to unify the world under Greek language and culture—a process we know as hellenization. This practice continued to a varying extent under his successors and reached its height under Antiochus Epiphanes, who came to power in 175 BC. He began a policy of radical hellenization under which he determined to eradicate the Jewish religion. This sets the scene for the events described in 1 Maccabees, our next narrative book, and for the final Old Testament period: the Maccabean Revolt.

At stake during this time is not merely the Jews' allegiance to the crown but their very identity as the people of God. Under Antiochus, the Temple becomes home to sexual revels and pagan sacrifices. Anyone who openly practices his faith, whether by observing the Sabbath or a Jewish feast, or circumcising his son, or even so much as calling himself a Jew, risks torture and death. A turning point comes when a faithful priest named Mattathias refuses to sacrifice to Zeus and kills a man who does. A 24-year revolt led by his son, Judas Maccabeus, follows and helps establish political and religious independence for Judah until Rome takes control of the area in 63 BC. Three years into the revolt, the Temple is taken back and cleansed. According to the Talmud, oil that was only enough for one lamp lasted miraculously eight days. The event is commemorated today as Hanukah—the Festival of Lights. The miracle of the oil, while not recorded in Scripture, gives us our color for this period: orange, for the light in the lamps.

1 Maccabees provides a history of the leadership and battles of the Maccabees (and the Hasmonean dynasty) during the 2nd century BC, but it is not merely an historical account. Its greater purpose is to showcase the providence and protection of God and the importance of staying true to the Covenant even to death. This period helps to set the scene for the fulfillment of God's promises in the New Testament. With the Maccabean Revolt, the Old Testament periods end on a high note with great examples of courage and faith.

**DAY 74**

Date_____

1 Maccabees ☐ 1    ☐ 2    ☐ 3    ☐ 4

*With the restoration of the Temple in Jerusalem, there was once more a place for God in Jerusalem, a visible sign of his presence among His people.*

JOURNAL

*Define the threat Israel faces in chapter 1.*

*What do Mattathias and his sons accomplish?*

*Before he dies, Mattathias uses the example of the faithful greats who went before them to strengthen his sons in their faith. How might their example strengthen you?*

*Notice what Judas Maccabeus depends upon to win against armies far greater than his own.*

**74**

?

*The eight-day celebration described in 4:56 is commemorated today in the Jewish Festival of Lights, or Hanukkah.*

## PRAYER

Mattathias and his sons stood up against the threats of Hellenization:

Help us resist worldliness in our culture and follow only you.

DAY
75

Date_____

1 Maccabees ☐ 5 ☐ 6 ☐ 7 ☐ 8

2 Maccabees 7 tells of seven brothers and their mother whose firm faith held them steadfast to the death during the early years of this period.

*To what does Antiochus attribute his end? (chapter 6)*

*After the death of Antiochus, Lysias governs for two years in the name of the King's young son. Afraid of being overthrown, he extends an offer of peace to the Jews, which he promptly breaks.*

*In these chapters we see the wane of Greece's influence and the rise of Rome. In chapter 8, the Jews make an alliance of friendship with Rome. Why?*

**?**

## PRAYER

Mattathias and his sons stood up against the threats of Hellenization:

Help us resist worldliness in our culture and follow only you.

**DAY 76**

Date_____

1 Maccabees   ☐ 9   ☐ 10   ☐ 11   ☐ 12

The wall around the inner court of the sanctuary, which is partially torn down in 9:54, is the wall separating the Jews from the Gentiles. Read Ephesians 2:14 to see how the breaking down of that wall takes on an entirely new meaning after the death and resurrection of Jesus Christ.

*Don't feel you need to get all the details; just read to get the general drift of how Judah fares in relationship to its neighbors.*

*With the close of chapter 9, there is again a man of Israel ruling the people of Judah: Jonathan, brother of Judas Maccabeus. He is not a king but a judge like those in the book of Judges.*

*What contribution does Jonathan make to Jerusalem? In chapter 10 Jonathan is appointed High Priest by King Alexander (son of Antiochus Epiphanes and backed by Rome).*

**?**

_____
_____
_____
_____
_____
_____
_____
_____
_____
_____

_____
_____
_____
_____
_____
_____

## PRAYER

Mattathias and his sons stood up against the threats of Hellenization:

Help us resist worldliness in our culture and follow only you.

DAY
77

Date_____

1 Maccabees  ☐ 13   ☐ 14   ☐ 15   ☐ 16

In 63 BC, Rome intervened when two brothers fought for the throne. The battle ended with Hyrcanus II in power but with Judah a Roman protectorate. Hasmonean rule ended in 37 BC when the pro-Roman Herod the Great was made king of the Jews.

*After Jonathan's death, his brother Simon leads the Jews. Notice the poem to the glory of Simon in chapter 14.*

*Simon becomes supreme leader of the Jews under Roman authority. He is named high priest, governor, and Ethnarch. That the roles of king and priest are combined in one man is unique to this time. Simon Maccabees' son John Hyrcanus served, like his father, as both king and high priest. He is the founder of the Hasmonean dynasty.*

**77**

JOURNAL

## PRAYER

Mattathias and his sons stood up against the threats of Hellenization:

Help us resist worldliness in our culture and follow only you.

# MESSIANIC FULFILLMENT

*Gold*

*"Do not be afraid, Mary, for you have found favor with God. And behold, you will conceive in your womb and bear a son, and you shall call his name Jesus. He will be great, and will be called the Son of the Most High; and the Lord God will give to him the throne of his father David, and he will reign over the house of Jacob for ever; and of his kingdom there will be no end" (Lk. 1:30-33).*

# INTRODUCTION *to*
# MESSIANIC FULFILLMENT

◆ ◆ ◆ ◆ ◆ ◆ ◆ ◆ ◆ ◆ ◇ ◆

**Narrative book:** Luke

**Color:** Gold / the gifts of the Magi

**Key people and events:**

| | |
|---|---|
| • The Annunciation | Luke 1:26-38 |
| • Jesus' birth and childhood | Luke 2 |
| • John baptizes Jesus | Luke 3:21-22 |
| • Jesus tempted in the desert | Luke 4 |
| • Sermon on the Mount | Luke 6:20-49 |
| • Last Supper | Luke 22:1-38 |
| • Passion | Luke 22-23 |
| • Resurrection | Luke 24:1-12 |
| • Ascension | Luke 24:44-53 |

The period of *Maccabean Revolt* draws a curtain on the Old Testament. "Testament" is our English translation of the Greek word that itself translates the Hebrew word for "covenant." It refers to the covenant promises through which God bound Israel to Himself as His people. In the covenants He made with Abraham, Moses, and David, God promised to give Israel the land of Canaan and to make her a kingdom ruled from an everlasting throne by a king in the line of David. That kingdom, it was promised, would be a source of blessing to the entire world. That covenant becomes "Old" when the one to whom the promises point—the Messiah, and his reign—comes to make a new and everlasting covenant.

As God told the people through His prophet Jeremiah during the time of the exile, this new covenant is "not like the covenant which I made with their fathers when I took them by the hand to bring them out of the land of Egypt, my covenant which they broke, though I was their husband, says the LORD. But this is the covenant which I will make with the house of Israel after those days, says the LORD: I will put my law within them, and I will write it upon their hearts; and I will be their God, and they shall be my people" (Jeremiah 31:32-33).

This new covenant will not do away with the old, it will fulfill it. The things we have already seen come to pass—the conquest of the land, the establishment of the kingdom, and so on—turn out to be temporal signposts pointing to the much greater spiritual reality of the Kingdom of God that His Son comes to establish. Even God's presence with His people in the Temple turns out to be just a foreshadowing of the new Temple, Jesus Christ, in whom God Himself comes to dwell on Earth. (And that, in turn, looks ahead to the presence of God through the Holy Spirit in individual believers. We have yet to see the ultimate fulfillment that will be revealed in heaven.)

Humanly speaking, as we move from the Old Testament to the New, things do not look good for Israel. The Jews may be home but in a sense they are still "slaves" subject to foreign empires. Spiritually speaking, they remain exiled by sin. They wait in longing for the coming of the Messiah. But when Israel looks to be at its weakest, God will change everything.

The period of *Messianic Fulfillment* is represented by the color gold, which can be remembered by the gift of gold given by the Magi to the Christ child. We will read the story as it is told in the gospel of Luke.

**DAY 78**

Date_____

Luke ☐ 1 ☐ 2 ☐ 3 ☐ 4

*Mary is the new Eve. With her obedient "yes," she undid the "knot" of Eve's disobedience. And it is her seed that will crush the head of the Serpent, fulfilling the curse God put on the Serpent in the Garden of Eden.*

*The angel Gabriel last appeared in Scripture during the exile, when he said that though it would last just 70 years, Israel would continue in 490 years of spiritual exile (Daniel 9). Those 490 years are up!*

*What do these witnesses tell about who Jesus is and why he has come? God; Zechariah; Simeon; John the Baptist; demons.*

*Each phrase Jesus uses to silence the Devil is taken from the story of Israel's wanderings, from a time when they failed to trust God. These words were given them so they would know how to defeat temptation and live in trust. How can they help you do the same?*

**78**

JOURNAL

*Jesus' words in 4:16-21 announce the long-awaited Jubilee, a year when slaves are set free, debts cancelled, and ancestral property returned. He is ushering in a new return from spiritual exile.*

## PRAYER

You sent your only Son, Jesus Christ the Messiah, to fulfill all your promises:

Give us new life in him.

DAY
79

Date_____

Luke ☐ 5 ☐ 6 ☐ 7 ☐ 8

*Jesus' sermon in chapter 6 shows him as a "new Moses" giving God's law to His people. The original law taught freed slaves to live as free children of God. In Christ, we achieve a greater freedom: freedom from sin.*

*After being tempted in the desert down South near Jerusalem, Jesus returned to Galilee (up North) by the power of the Holy Spirit. The description of his ministry there continues through chapter 9.*

*What types of actions characterize Jesus' ministry?*

*What is the focus of Jesus' "Sermon on the Plain" in chapter 6? How does it speak to you?*

**79**

JOURNAL

**?**

*Jesus' message that humility and love of enemies will usher in the kingdom was radically new to a people expecting to establish an earthly kingdom through military means.*

## PRAYER

You sent your only Son, Jesus Christ the Messiah, to fulfill all your promises:

Give us new life in him.

DAY
80

Date_____

Luke     ☐ 9     ☐ 10     ☐ 11     ☐ 12

_Moses and Elijah speak with Jesus of the "exodus" whereby he will pass through a sea of suffering and lead his people through death to sin and to a new life in him. Keep this mission in mind as you read._

*According to Jesus, what are the conditions and cost of discipleship?*

*Who is Jesus revealed to be in the Transfiguration?*

*In 9:51, Jesus "sets his face to go to Jerusalem." There will be no turning back from this point. The next ten chapters describe his ministry in Judea (previously "Judah"), during which time he establishes the foundation of his kingdom.*

**80**

JOURNAL

**?**

*At the burning bush, God revealed His name: "I AM." Not until Jesus comes as Son, is God revealed as Father (read Galatians 4:7 to see how that applies to us). The Lord's Prayer asks us to recognize this and act on it.*

## PRAYER

You sent your only Son, Jesus Christ the Messiah, to fulfill all your promises:

Give us new life in him.

# DAY 81

Date_____

Luke ☐ 13 ☐ 14 ☐ 15 ☐ 16

*When Hellenization began to threaten, some of the Jews drew apart into a distinct class of "separated ones," the Pharisees. They focused on personal piety and were devoted to the Law. By the time of Christ, they were the religious experts and sources of teaching and authority.*

**81**

Jesus explains the kingdom of God by telling parables. Note the things that you learn from those in chapters 13 and 14. (Where is it? Who is invited? Who will get in?)

Meditate on Jesus' sayings on discipleship in 14:25-33. What do they say to you?

Notice the message common to the three parables Jesus tells in Luke 15. What do these parables illustrate about God?

**?**

The Prodigal Son is a picture of Israel in exile, squandering her inheritance.

## PRAYER

You sent your only Son, Jesus Christ the Messiah, to fulfill all your promises:

Give us new life in him.

DAY
82

Date_____

Luke    ❑ 17    ❑ 18    ❑ 19    ❑ 20

*The Sadducees became the dominant priestly party some time after the Maccabean Revolt. They tended to be wealthy political leaders who allied themselves with Greece and Rome. They were fiercely opposed by the Pharisees, who advocated a strict separatism.*

In 18:31-34, Jesus predicts His passion for the third time. How do the disciples respond? Will they be prepared for his death?

In chapter 19, Jesus rides into Jerusalem on a donkey, in the manner of a king riding to his coronation.

The testing of Jesus picks up in chapter 20 as religious leaders question his authority.

**82**

JOURNAL

**?**

## PRAYER

You sent your only Son, Jesus Christ the Messiah, to fulfill all your promises:

Give us new life in him.

DAY
83

Date_____

Luke    ☐ 21    ☐ 22    ☐ 23    ☐ 24

*In his suffering, Christ takes upon himself the curse of Adam (the toil; the thorns; the sweat) and the curse of death. By pouring himself out in love to death, he saves. He takes on our curse and offers us his life.*

The disciples couldn't conceive of a suffering Messiah, yet Christ came for that very purpose. Today's reading shows him heading resolutely for the Cross. Watch to see how Jesus does what Adam failed to do.

*What echoes do you see in the Last Supper (22:14-20) of things in the Old Testament?*

*What kind of man is Peter, the man Jesus chooses to be the foundation of his Church?*

?

*Even with the penalty paid for sin, the problems remain of our broken nature, the loss of grace, and the tendency to sin that all inherit from Adam. Jesus' mission is not complete without his resurrection, which assures us we can trust the Father. Read Romans 6:5 to see why.*

## PRAYER

You sent your only Son, Jesus Christ the Messiah, to fulfill all your promises:

Give us new life in him.

# THE CHURCH

*White*

"But you shall receive power when the Holy Spirit has come upon you; and you shall be my witnesses in Jerusalem and in all Judea and Sama'ria and to the end of the earth" (Ac. 1:8).

# INTRODUCTION *to the* CHURCH

◆   ◆   ◆   ◆   ◆   ◆   ◆   ◆   ◆   ◆   ◆   ◇

**Narrative book:**  Acts of the Apostles

**Color:**  White / the spotless Bride of Christ

**Key people and events:**

| | |
|---|---|
| • Witness in Jerusalem (33-35 AD) | Acts 1 – 8 |
| • Pentecost | Acts 2:1-13 |
| • Choosing of the Seven (Diaconate) | Acts 6:1-7 |
| • Stephen martyred | Acts 6 – 7 |
| • Witness in Judea and Samaria (35-45 AD) | Acts 8 – 13 |
| • Saul's conversion | Acts 9 |
| • Cornelius's vision | Acts 10 |
| • Peter's arrest and deliverance | Acts 12 |
| • Witness to the ends of the earth (45-62 AD) | Acts 13 – 28 |
| • Paul's 1st missionary journey | Acts 13 – 14 |
| • Council of Jerusalem (49 AD) | Acts 15 |
| • Paul's 2nd missionary journey | Acts 15:36–18:22 |
| • Paul's 3rd missionary journey | Acts 18:23–21:16 |

In the period of *Messianic Fulfillment*, we reached the pinnacle of our journey, the climax toward which the entire story has pointed. Who would have guessed that God Himself would come to Earth as a man, or that He would suffer and die so that the demands of the covenant would be met and all His scattered children could be reunited in Him? Who would have guessed that Satan's fiercest weapons—suffering and death—would be transformed into the very door to eternal life? It is hard to fathom the depths of God's love for us.

It would seem that the story is over. The promises are fulfilled, the problems solved. And yet something very important remains. The disciples Jesus left on Earth, and all those who follow, are invited to become part of the story and enter into the new kingdom that Jesus founded here and which will reach its own perfect fulfillment in heaven at the end of time. "This is the new covenant in my blood," he said at the Last Supper. God has been building his family through covenants since the start of the story. Now the whole world will be invited in.

The final stage of the *Great Adventure* is *The Church*, which is the earthly embodiment of the eternal Kingdom of God. Its birth and early years are described in the book of Acts. We remember it by the color white for the spotless Bride of Christ. In the same way that white light from the sun is made up of all the colors of the rainbow, in the white light of the Church can be found all the colors of the preceding periods. In it is the culmination of the entire story.

Acts 1:8 provides us with a structure for our reading: "But you shall receive power when the Holy Spirit has come upon you; and you shall be my witnesses in Jerusalem and in all Judea and Sama'ria and to the end of the earth." This describes three "waves of witness" that begin in the city of Jerusalem and expand outward as the Apostles and other disciples proclaim the good news of the Gospel farther and farther afield.

As you read, notice that the Church is founded on the 12 apostles (representing the 12 tribes of Israel); is empowered with the life of Christ by the Holy Spirit; expands to include not just children of Israel but Gentiles as well; and thrives despite (and even because of!) fierce opposition. You also might notice that just as Christ lived out the life of Israel during his time on earth (only doing right what they failed to do), now he acts through his body the Church. Look for specific ways in which first the apostles and then other Christian disciples live out the life of Christ. Their lives provide a model for ours.

DAY
84

Date_____

Acts  ☐ 1   ☐ 2   ☐ 3   ☐ 4

*The Feast of Pentecost is the antithesis of the Tower of Babel, when languages were confused and people scattered. Now the scattered nations will be gathered back into God's family.*

*Notice the word "began" in 1:1. Acts tells what Jesus continues to do, after his ascension to heaven, through His body, the Church.*

*What do the apostles do that Jesus also did while He was on earth?*

*Watch for changes in the disciples after they receive the Holy Spirit.*

*What does the early church community look like?*

84

JOURNAL

## PRAYER

The Church carries on your work in the world:

Make us faithful ambassadors of your love.

DAY
85

Date_____

Acts     ☐ 5     ☐ 6     ☐ 7     ☐ 8

*What do you learn from the story of Ananias and Sapphira?*

*Deacons are first appointed in chapter 6.*

*Stephen's defense in Acts 7 reveals Israel's consistent rejection of God's leaders and their misunderstanding of the role of the Temple.*

*What is the result of the persecution that breaks out in chapter 8?*

85

JOURNAL

## PRAYER

The Church carries on your work in the world:

Make us faithful ambassadors of your love.

DAY
86

Date_____

Acts     ☐ 9     ☐ 10     ☐ 11     ☐ 12

Today's reading covers the wave of witness in Judea and Samaria (South and North Palestine). The key people to watch are Saul/ Paul and Peter.

Who does Saul discover he has really been persecuting? What does that mean about the life of Jesus Christ?

Notice the means God uses to convince Peter and others of one of the central truths of the new kingdom, that it is open to **anyone.**

86

JOURNAL

? _____
_____
_____
_____
_____
_____
_____
_____
_____
_____
_____

_____
_____
_____
_____
_____
_____

## PRAYER

The Church carries on your work in the world:

Make us faithful ambassadors of your love.

**DAY**
**87**

Date_____

Acts        ☐ 13      ☐ 14      ☐ 15      ☐ 16

_On Paul's first missionary journey, he establishes a number of churches. In his second and third journeys, he returns to instruct and strengthen them._

JOURNAL

87

*Herod's persecution sends the apostles beyond Palestine to witness
"to the ends of the earth."*

*In each city, where do the missionaries go first?
When do they move on to preach to others?*

*What serious dispute is raised by the conversion of the Gentiles? This
dispute is resolved in the "Jerusalem Council" (chapter 15). Notice the
ruling of the council and how is it communicated to the new churches.*

?

## PRAYER

The Church carries on your work in the world:

Make us faithful ambassadors of your love.

DAY
88

Date_____

Acts        ❏ 17     ❏ 18     ❏ 19     ❏ 20

---

_Paul wrote to the church at Corinth about love in some of the most beautiful words recorded in Scripture. You can read them in 1 Corinthians 13._

*Paul's speech at the Areopagus in Athens (chapter 17) is notable for the way he uses their beliefs as a starting point for his message. How can you use that same approach in communicating the gospel?*

*What cities did Paul visit during his third journey (starting in 18:23), and how did he fare in each?*

*Watch the way Paul works to establish the leaders of the church at Ephesus at the end of chapter 20.*

**88**

**?**

*Read Paul's letters to the churches in the context of the narrative framework provided by his missionary journeys.*

## PRAYER

The Church carries on your work in the world:

Make us faithful ambassadors of your love.

DAY
89

Date_____

Acts  ☐ 21  ☐ 22  ☐ 23  ☐ 24

The rest of Acts has to do with Paul's arrest and imprisonment in Caesarea and the trials that lead to his journey to Rome and ministry there.

What in Paul's testimony in Acts 22 most arouses the Jews' anger?

How does Paul turn a disagreement between the Pharisees and Sadducees to his own advantage?

Watch for the way Jesus strengthens Paul in Acts 23.

## PRAYER

The Church carries on your work in the world:

Make us faithful ambassadors of your love.

DAY
90

Date_____

Acts     ☐ 25     ☐ 26     ☐ 27     ☐ 28

*According to Tradition, both Peter and Paul were martyred in Rome during Nero's persecution of the Christians c. 64 AD. It is said that St. Paul was beheaded and that St. Peter was crucified (with his head downward, at his own request).*

*How does Paul pass on the courage he has received from Christ during the storm of chapter 27?*

*Paul is taken to Rome, where he remains for two years under house arrest but freely preaching the kingdom of God.*

*While this completes the final narrative book of the Bible, it by no means closes the period of The Church. The story that began with a rupture in God's family has found its solution in God's Son. How is that story continuing in your life?*

?

*The death of Peter and Paul did not bring an end to the church, but in some way spurred it on. Truly "the blood of the martyrs is the seed of the church" (Tertullian).*

## PRAYER

The Church carries on your work in the world:

Make us faithful ambassadors of your love.